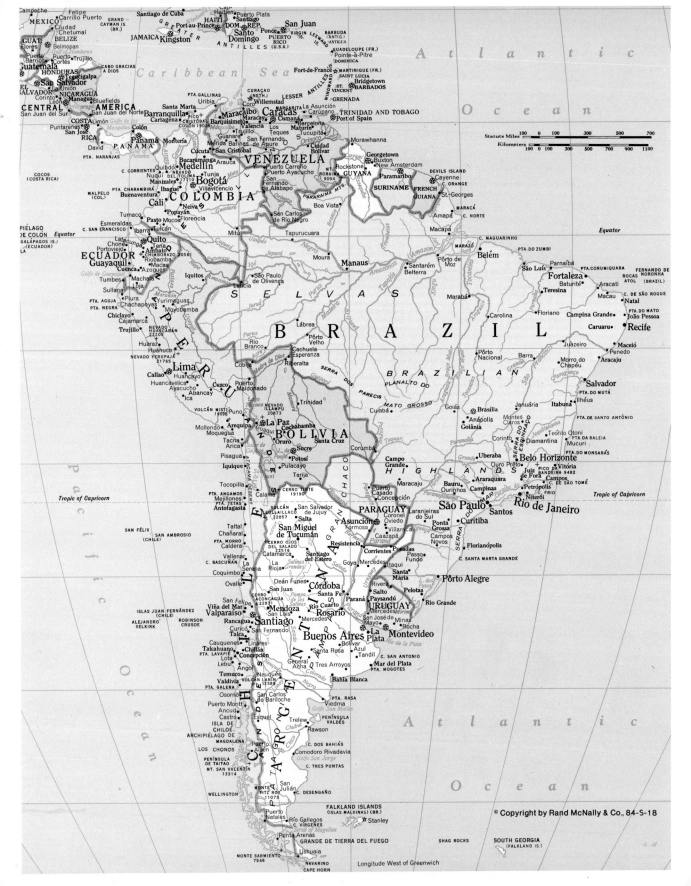

Enchantment of the World

BRAZIL

By Wilbur and Susanna Cross

Consultant for Brazil: João Francisco Bezerra, Translator, Professor of Portuguese, Brazilian-American Cultural Institute, Washington, D.C.

Consultant for Reading: Robert L. Hillerich, Ph.D., Bowling Green State University, Bowling Green, Ohio

CHILDRENS PRESS ™

CHICAGO

Samba dancers in elaborate costumes are featured during carnival.

Picture Acknowledgments
Hillstrom Stock Photos/© **Milt and Joan Mann,** Cover, 4, 43 (right), 44, 45 (2 photos), 46 (left), 52 (right), 72, 83 (2 photos), 88, 99, 104 (top left and bottom right), 113, 115; © **Liz Veternick,** 43 (left), 103
Tom Stack & Associates/© **Gary Milburn,** 16 (left); © **Steve Martin,** 17 (right); © **Don Rutledge,** 39, 62, (left), 68 (top)
Historical Pictures Service, Chicago: 28, 33, 34
© **Victor Banks:** 14, 19, 21, 81, 84
© **Reynolds Photographers:** 5, 22, 42 (bottom right), 46 (right), 110 (left)
United Press International: 37, 38
© **John M. Hunter for Reynolds Photographers/**6, 9, 12, 16 (right), 31, 40 (top), 42 (top right and bottom left), 48 (middle left, bottom), 55, 59 (left), 62 (right), 65, 66, 78 (right), 96 (2 photos), 104
© **Victor Englebert:** 10, 51 (2 photos), 58 (2 photos), 93 (2 photos), 107 (2 photos), 110 (right)
© **Robert Perron:** 11, 60, 79, 104 (bottom left)
Nawrocki Stock Photo/© **Mark Gamba,** 40 (bottom), 101
Root Resources/© **Grace H. Lanctot,** 17 (left), 42 (top left), 67; © **Jane P. Downton,** 102
© **Chandler Forman/**59 (right), 114
© **Virginia Grimes/**25, 75 (left), 86
© **Chip and Rosa Maria Peterson/**48 (top, middle right), 52 (left), 54, 56, 57 (2 photos), 68, 75 (right), 78 (left), 85, 90
Courtesy Flag Research Center, Winchester, Massachusetts 01890/Flag on back cover
Cover: Sugar Loaf Mountain and Bay of Guanabara, Rio de Janeiro

Library of Congress Cataloging in Publication Data

Cross, Wilbur.
  Brazil.

  (Enchantment of the world)
  Includes index.
  Summary: An introduction to the geography, history, economy, natural resources, people, and culture of the vast and diverse South American country that is the fifth largest nation in the world.
    1. Brazil—Juvenile literature. [1. Brazil]
I. Cross, Susanna. II. Title. III. Series.
F2508.5.C76 1984   981   84-7621
ISBN 0-516-02753-0   AACR2

EIGHTH PRINTING, 1994.

Cane market in Salvador, Brazil

TABLE OF CONTENTS

Beach at Bahia (Salvador). This was the first place colonized by the Portuguese.

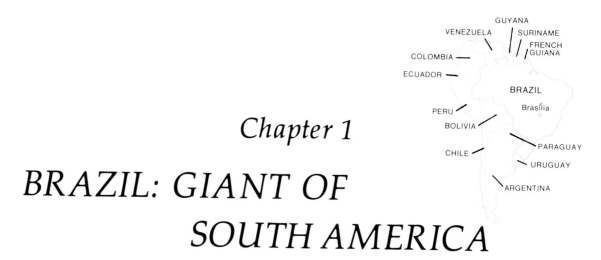

Chapter 1

BRAZIL: GIANT OF SOUTH AMERICA

The fifth largest nation in the world, Brazil occupies nearly half of the total area of South America. It borders on every other country on the continent except Chile and Ecuador. It is a land of dramatic contrasts, ranging from the deepest jungles and wildest frontiers to vast farmlands, ultramodern cities, and thousands of miles of magnificent coastline. Historically and culturally, Brazil presents a rich blend of ancient civilizations, primitive races, and cultivated traditions.

With a landmass of more than three million square miles (larger than all of Europe) and a broad diversity of characteristics, Brazil is really five countries in one. Thus, it has been divided into five regions, each with its own distinguishing features. Yet, despite the marked differences from one region to another and the enormous breadth of the country, Brazil does not present wide extremes of topography or altitude. The country can, in fact, be described as a land of elevated plateaus, low plains, and extensive basins, with very few areas that are more than a thousand feet above sea level.

SOUTH AMERICA WITH A DIFFERENCE

One of the basic differences between Brazil and all other Latin countries in the Americas is that the official language is Portuguese, not Spanish. Also unlike its neighbors in South America, Brazil has no substantial regional dialects or racial pockets. If there is one word that best describes Brazil, it is *unity*. There is a unity of language, religion, habits, and customs that contradicts the fact that this vast country was colonized by diverse groups almost from its beginnings early in the sixteenth century.

Politically, Brazil has been difficult to define. The country has been many things: a Portuguese colony, a kingdom, an independent monarchy, a republic, a dictatorship, a military dependency, and a democracy. Officially, it is known as the Federative Republic of Brazil, a name that recognizes both its central power and its dependence upon individual states and territories. Governments have formed, prospered, failed, and been replaced by a succession of leaders with widely differing political beliefs and backgrounds.

Yet, despite their political differences and frequent upheavals, sometimes violent in nature, the many governments have had surprisingly similar goals. Basically, their objectives have been to keep the country unified, develop the immense natural resources, promote commerce and industry, integrate the vast stretches of the interior with the coastal regions, improve agricultural production, and link cities and towns with an effective communication and transportation network. As governments have come and gone, some of the goals have come close to realization. Others have remained as knotty challenges for the future. Yet the national unity has persisted and continues to be

Cattle graze in tropical wetlands.

one of the dominating characteristics of this exuberant nation.

Most non-Brazilians recognize only a few of Brazil's most important features: Rio de Janeiro, claimed by many to be the most beautiful city in the world; Brasília, the most modern capital in the Western Hemisphere; the Amazon River, scene of more adventure stories than perhaps any other place on earth; and the dense jungles of the interior, which are more fearful to imagine than the heart of Africa. Eventually, this lack of familiarity with a nation that is the home of over 160 million people must be corrected. For Brazil is a vitally important nation, with a potential for future development that is overwhelming.

Since 93 percent of Brazil's territory lies below the equator, its seasons are just the opposite of those in North America and Europe. While North Americans suffer through the winter months, for example, Brazil enjoys its long, hot summer. Even at the height of the Brazilian winter (June to September), the climate ranges in most areas from the tropical to the temperate.

Yanomami Indian children swim in the Tootobi River surrounded by the Amazon rain forest.

Brazil has seven distinct types of vegetation. In the south are the forests and the grasslands. In the Pantanal region to the southwest, there is a unique floodplain, a mixture of wet savannas and palms. Most of the interior is covered with woodland savannas, known as *campo cerrado* and suitable for crops only when properly plowed and fertilized. To the north is the great rain forest, known as the *selva*, where the foliage is thick and the rainfall incessant. Scattered around the country are deciduous forests, which go through the familiar cycles of leaf growth and shedding. Lastly, there is the region known as the *várzea*, great plains in the north that are regularly covered by floodwaters, making them among the most fertile lands in South America.

THE POPULATION EXPLOSION

Since the middle of the twentieth century, Brazil's population has been increasing rapidly, mainly because of the high birthrate. The result is a nation of people who are young in spirit, as well as in age. At least 35 percent of the population today is made up of people under the age of fifteen while nearly 58 percent range between fifteen and fifty-nine years of age.

Brazil is a melting pot of races. Its racial heritage can be seen in the faces of its citizens.

One of the major problems of Brazilian leaders during the past three decades has been to make life in the interior more attractive. They want to stem the tide of people moving to the cities like Rio, São Paulo, Belo Horizonte, and Recife and attract them to sparsely populated regions that have great economic potential for the country.

Like the United States, Brazil was once described as a "melting pot" of human races. Over the years, immigrants from North America, Europe, Africa, and Asia have included Italians, who helped to develop agriculture (particularly the coffee industry); Germans, who settled in the south; Japanese, who began producing vegetable crops in farm belts near the large cities; Spaniards (from Europe and neighboring countries alike), who were attracted to the Portuguese-Old World culture; and even African blacks, who originally arrived as slaves to replace the natives captured in the Amazonian and Mato Grosso jungles.

Some of these ethnic groups continue to survive and flourish. Others have been completely assimilated into the Portuguese culture and the typical Brazilian way of life.

As you will see, Brazil is unlike any other country in South America or, for that matter, the world.

A coastal plain near the city of Vitória in the state of Esperitu Santo

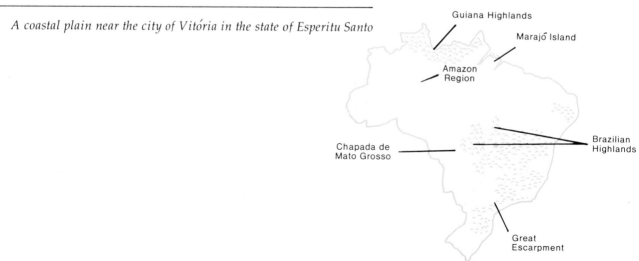

Guiana Highlands

Marajó Island

Amazon Region

Chapada de Mato Grosso

Brazilian Highlands

Great Escarpment

Chapter 2

THE FACE OF A NATION

The silhouette of Brazil bears a striking resemblance to the continent in which it lies. Like South America, Brazil is broad and fan-shaped at the top, narrowing down to a kind of "handle" at the southern tip.

Although Brazil is ringed by neighboring countries that have some of the highest, most forbidding peaks in the Americas, the country itself has few mountains, and none that can compare with the Andes to the west. In fact, almost half of the nation's territory consists of plains and lowlands, averaging only a few hundred feet above sea level. These include the great Amazon Basin in the north, the La Plata Basin along the River Plate in the south and southwest, and a comparatively narrow coastal strip that runs along the Atlantic Ocean on the east. The rest of the landscape consists of the vast Central Plateau (Brazilian Highlands), south of the Amazon, and the Guiana Highlands, north of the Amazon. The latter lie only partly in Brazil.

The Guiana and Brazilian highlands date from the early Precambrian period. They are among the oldest formations on earth, formed almost four billion years ago. In structure, they follow a pattern of hilly uplands, with low mountains rather than rugged peaks. One reason why the mountains are not higher is

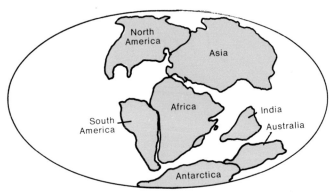

Cattle are raised on the Pantanal, a low-lying region near the Paraguay River.

that the Precambrian rocks tend to weather rapidly and are constantly subjected to the heavy tropical rains, which carry off the soils and sediments. Few of the ranges are more than 2,000 feet (610 meters) in height.

More recent mountain formations follow parts of the eastern coastline, where they drop sharply toward the sea to form a series of cliffs, called the Serra do Mar (backbone of the sea). These cliffs form a clear dividing line between the hills and the rich coastal plain. The plain, which is very narrow, runs from the northeastern tip of the country, near Natal, to Porto Alegre in the south. There the plain fans out to form the Campanha Gaúcha, the lowlands of the state of Rio Grande do Sul.

Located in the southwestern region of Brazil is another plain, the Pantanal. This low-lying region, which is periodically flooded by the Paraguay River, is used largely for cattle raising.

Geologists have noted the surprising similarities between much of the Brazilian terrain and that of South Africa. This is explained

14

by the continental drift theory, which holds that the continents on the earth's surface have changed positions considerably through geologic time. It is believed that Africa and South America were one supercontinent until the Paleozoic era, 225 million years ago, when they broke apart and began a slow drift to their present positions. This theory is supported by the fact that the coast of Brazil and the Gulf of Guinea in Africa, opposite each other across the Atlantic Ocean, form a "jigsaw fit." In other words, if some immense force were to push them together, they would line up exactly, like the pieces in a jigsaw puzzle.

NORTHERN REGION: THE EXOTIC AMAZON

About one half of Brazil, lying in the north and northwest, consists of the Amazon plain, which separates the Guiana Highlands from the Central Plateau. The plain is formed by a series of low plateaus that descend gradually towards the Amazon River. This is one of the wildest, most uncivilized areas on earth, an area of 1,380,722 square miles (3,576,070 square kilometers) of rain forests, swamps, rivers, and jungles. Most travel has to be by boat, by helicopter, or on the few roads that have been hacked through the jungles at great cost, both in money and human lives.

Nature rules the Amazon plain, dominating everything else. The rivers, forests, and swamps dictate the style of life of all who live or travel there. As a result, the region is more sparsely populated than almost any other on earth. Ironically, it holds enormous fascination for humans, especially for the explorers and adventurers who have attempted to tame its wilderness.

For animals, birds, plants, and other wildlife, the Amazon plain is an exotic Eden. Its lush tropical forests and its rain-fed rivers

Two-toed sloths and giant lily pads can be found in the Amazon.

are homes to some seven hundred species of mammals and eighteen hundred varieties of birds. Its rivers and swamps, which contain the largest volume of fresh water in the world, are thought to have as many as fifteen hundred species of fish and other aquatic creatures. Many of these animals, birds, and fish are beautiful and colorful. Some are bizarre; others are almost grotesque. Some can be tamed easily as pets; others are poisonous, voracious, or otherwise dangerous to humans.

Of the twenty largest rivers in the world, ten run through the Amazon Basin. The most famous and the second longest in the world is the mighty Amazon River. The river starts in the Peruvian Andes and flows eastward 4,087 miles (6,576 kilometers) to the Atlantic Ocean. For 1,962 miles (3,158 kilometers) it passes through Brazil to its mouth. There the river spreads for 180 miles (290

Aerial view of the Amazon River near Manaus (left). Like many of the Amazon's wildlife, this St. Vincent Amazon parrot is an endangered species.

kilometers) and flows around an island, Marajó, which is larger than Switzerland. The force of the river as it enters the sea causes tidal waves twelve feet (3.7 meters) high and mingles the salt waters of the Atlantic with the fresh river waters for 200 miles (322 kilometers) offshore.

The Amazon is the highway to the vast interior. It is navigable upstream by seagoing ships for over 2,000 miles (3,218 kilometers) and by small boats for hundreds of miles beyond that. The region along the river was once the world's major source of rubber.

Several rich cities were built along the Amazon and even today visitors can see traces of the immense wealth rubber brought to these cities.

The Amazon forest that enfolds the river is important. It is said to be responsible for replenishing about half of the world's supply of oxygen. Oxygen is released by both living and decaying plants in great abundance. Since the jungles of the Amazon region are almost solid with plant life and since the rate of growth and decay is extremely high, oxygen is released in enormous volumes. Also, since there are no seasonal changes and no cold weather to impede the process, the production of oxygen continues year after year without interruption.

NORTHEAST REGION: THE GOLDEN COAST

The origins of Brazil itself lie along the upper Atlantic coast. It was here that the early colonizers first developed a new trade, having discovered a native tree with wood as red as a glowing coal. Its color could be readily extracted for the making of paints and dyes. Actually named *pau-brasil* but called "bresel wood" by the Europeans, this commodity was what gave Brazil its name.

The northeast region, with land rich and fertile and days sunny and warm, was the site of the first sugarcane fields. The land along the more than 2,000 miles (3,218 kilometers) of coast that make up part of this region includes many sandy beaches, palm forests, and low headlands with thick foliage and outcroppings of weathered rock. A number of great forests are here, too, mainly in Rio Grande do Norte, on the northeastern curve of the region, and in the territory of Maranhão to the west.

The Golden Coast was so named not only because of the income it produced during the early colonial ventures but also because of the beautiful coastline that attracts vacationers from home and abroad. The beaches and lagoons ringed with palms are distinctly tropical in nature. Some are protected by long barrier reefs, similar to those found along the shores of Australia. Recife, one of

Cliffs of Planalto in western Brazil

the major cities of the region, derives its name from the
Portuguese word for barrier reef, *arrecife*. Natural inlets,
connected by canals, are so much a part of the city's layout that it
has often been called the Brazilian Venice.

Inland, the terrain rises slightly to become plateaus that are arid
in nature, some with curious outcroppings of rock that have been
carved by nature over millions of years. One such formation has
been named The Seven Enchanted Cities because of its
resemblance to man-made structures. Seen from above, the rock
forms resemble small cities, arranged in streets and squares, with
castles, monuments, and tunnels. According to geologists, they
were caused by the erosion of wind and water. Superstitious
colonists believed, however, that they were made by Phoenician
explorers, who supposedly reached the coast more than two
thousand years ago.

CENTRAL-WEST REGION: THE WONDROUS WEST

The central-west region, with surprising environmental contrasts, stretches over a landmass of almost a million square miles (2.6 million square kilometers). Like its neighbor to the north, Amazonia, it is very wild and little explored in those sections of endless marshes traversed by the Araguaia River and vast stretches of pure jungle. It is most noted, environmentally, for a territory called the Pantanal, which is a floodplain and a reserve inhabited by millions of animals, birds, and fish. The plain covers more than 77,000 square miles (199,430 square kilometers), or an area nearly the size of former West Germany.

Along with the Amazon Basin, the Pantanal is one of the last virgin wildernesses on the face of the earth. Seen from a plane, the land resembles an enormous quilt made up of circles and ovals separated by patches of green and brown dots. These patterns, in shades of blue, green, and brown, are created by the thousands of ponds and marshes scattered across the lowland plains. Close up, it can be seen that the ground is covered by luxuriant blankets of rainbow-hued flowers, which bloom during the six-month rainy season from January to June.

In some sections, the Pantanal boasts lakes with crystal-clear waters that abound in game fish and attract sports fishermen from all over the globe. The shores are populated by rare and magnificent species of animals, including jaguars, wild boars, peccaries, and bobcats. Overhead, the skies are dotted with flocks of ducks, teals, pigeons, partridges, and herons. All of the animals and birds are protected by wild game laws, since this region is made up of several vast national parks.

The Araguaia River, which runs northward from the wild

Aerial view of a swamp in the Pantanal

Pantanal region, is one of the most unusual in South America. In length it is only a little more than a thousand miles (1,609 kilometers) — quite modest by Brazilian standards. But it attracts tremendous scientific interest because of its geological origins, its structure, and its reputation as the home of a greater variety of fish than any other river of any size. The waters of the Araguaia are unusually clear, and its shores are lined with innumerable natural beaches that are as soft and smooth as those found along the distant ocean. The Araguaia holds one further distinction — the site of Bananal, the largest river island in existence.

Finally, though hardly less significant, the central-west region includes the storied Mato Grosso savanna, another wilderness area whose interior has been visited by only handfuls of adventurous explorers. Although it is almost twice the size of Texas, the entire Mato Grosso has fewer than 1.8 million people, many of them Indians. Cuiabá, the state capital, lies at the geographic center of the South American continent.

Floodplains of Mato Grosso

Mato Grosso ("thick forest" in Portuguese) is an ecological wonderland of marshy terrain, thousands of lakes, and rivers of many sizes. Its lush landscape, with dazzling colors, is the home of countless species of birds. Here are the largest and most elegant herons, a Brazilian relative of the ostrich, and birds so unique that their Portuguese names have never been translated.

SOUTHEAST REGION: THE HEART OF BRAZIL

Geologically and geographically, there are few cities of any size that can compare favorably with Rio de Janeiro. Nothing can surpass the city's natural wonders. Its magnificent shoreline is indented by lagoons and bays of many sizes, from the tiny to the immense. Seaward, the ocean is dotted with islands. Inland, Rio has a backdrop of mountains, some with curiously sculptured peaks. Two of the most noted geological wonders are *Corcovado* (Hunchback) and *Pão de Açúcar* (Sugar Loaf), peaks that have come to be international symbols of the city itself. The former is 2,329 feet (710 meters) high, made dramatic by the enormous statue of Christ the Redeemer that stands with arms extended, overlooking the city. The latter is barely 1,300 feet (396 meters) high, but is formed of solid rock and affords a dramatic view of Guanabara Bay and other features in and around Rio.

The coastline to the south has the same abundance of beaches, lagoons, and islands. Inland, to the west of Rio, lie ranges of low but majestic mountains where a number of highland cities have been built. The tallest mountain in this southeast region is Pico da Bandeira, which stands at 9,482 feet (2,890 meters).

A little more than 100 miles (161 meters) to the southwest of Rio, the terrain is mountainous and heavily forested. This is the site of the Itatiaia National Park, an important ecological reserve of almost 26,000 acres (10,525 hectares). It abounds in wildlife, waterfalls, and uncommonly beautiful scenery. Within the park are five peaks that, although not nearly as high as Pico da Bandeira, offer good climbing and hiking.

Another important geological feature in the southeast region is the series of high plateaus located in the state of São Paulo. The city of São Paulo, the largest in South America, is built on such a plateau, some 2,600 feet (792 meters) above sea level. Because of its altitude and its location in the more temperate area of Brazil, the city enjoys an excellent climate.

To the north of São Paulo and west of Rio lies another plateau on which is built Belo Horizonte, Brazil's third largest city. Sitting at an altitude of 2,625 feet (800 meters) and ringed by mountains, it too enjoys a stimulating climate. Not far from Belo Horizonte, in Lapinha, is a unique natural wonder—a cave formed more than ten million years ago. Inside are the fossilized remains of a pre-

Columbian man. About 80 miles (129 kilometers) from the city is another cave structure, Maquiné, which contains almost 1,500 feet (457 meters) of passageways leading to seven enormous caverns filled with white, red, gray, and green stalagmites and stalactites.

Another type of natural wonder in the region is a series of scattered mineral springs and hot springs, which are supposed to have healing properties. Other such springs are scattered around Brazil, but most are found in this region.

THE SOUTHERN REGION: LAND OF CHARM

Geographically, the southern region resembles the handle of a Ping-Pong paddle, with all the rest of the country fanning out above it. It is bordered by Paraguay and Argentina to the west, Uruguay to the south, and the Atlantic Ocean to the east. This region is the only territory in Brazil where the four seasons of the year are readily distinguishable. It can be quite hot in the summer (January to March), moderate in the spring and fall, and cold in the winter (June to September). Snowfalls are not uncommon, particularly in the mountain areas.

The southern region consists primarily of flat plains and mountains. The plains, mostly on elevated plateaus, are excellent for raising cattle; the mountains are covered with forests. The coastline is much like that to the north, with many superb beaches and several long, narrow lagoons.

Perhaps the most notable geological feature of the region is Iguaçu Falls. Falling some 250 feet (76 meters) in a semicircle, it creates a rainbow and endless masses of white foam, as thousands of tons of water plunge into basins that have been hollowed by millions of years of erosion. Another natural

Iguaçu Falls—the footbridge at lip of falls allows visitors a closer look.

wonder, called *Sete Quedas* (the Seven Falls), is located at a point where the Iguaçu River is swallowed up by the Paraná River. Actually, there are nineteen waterfalls, some of which fall more than 300 feet (91 meters).

In the southern region the Itajaí Valley, located near the coast in the state of Santa Catarina, has an Old-World charm. The valley was settled by Germans more than 140 years ago, partly because the Itajaí River and surrounding land are reminiscent of Germany's Rhine River Valley.

The southernmost tip of Brazil, in the state of Rio Grande do Sul, would seem like home to visitors from the Great Plains region of the United States. This is a land of vast prairies, populated by *gaúchos,* the Brazilian counterpart of cowboys.

A FRIENDLY CLIMATE

Most of Brazil lies in the tropics. The equator runs through the northern region, just above the mouth of the Amazon River. The Tropic of Capricorn, the southern boundary of the tropics, runs through São Paulo, leaving only the southern "handle" of the country in the temperate zone. Yet the climate is comfortable in most regions of the country. Despite the image of the Amazon as a region of blistering heat, temperatures rarely climb into the 90s Fahrenheit (30s Celsius), largely because of the heavy rainfall that occurs during the hottest months of the year. The only section of Brazil that could be called torrid is in the northeast, where temperatures of 100 degrees Fahrenheit (38 degrees Celsius) are frequent.

Along the Atlantic coast, from Recife in the north to Rio de Janeiro, temperatures are seldom unbearable. In Rio, for example, the temperature in the warmest months (November through March) seldom rises above 80 degrees Fahrenheit (27 degrees Celsius) and in the coldest months rarely drops below 65 degrees Fahrenheit (18 degrees Celsius). To the north, sea breezes moderate the climate. Inland, especially in the central plains, the altitude keeps the temperatures lower than might be expected.

Rainfall is an important factor. Most of Brazil has moderate rainfall, with most of it occurring in the summers, between December and April. The winters generally tend to be dry and sunny. In the southern region, however, snow is a familiar winter sight, though it is seldom very heavy.

Although rainstorms can be extremely fierce in the interior and drought can sometimes be a problem, Brazil is happily free from hurricanes, cyclones, earthquakes, and similar disasters.

Chapter 3

AN OLD NEW-WORLD HISTORY

Legend has it that when Pedro Álvares Cabral, the Portuguese explorer, discovered Brazil in the year 1500 he thought he had anchored off the shores of an enormous island. Skeptical historians have said that Cabral and his experienced pilot were too skillful at navigation to have been so misled. Also, the Portuguese were aware that there were vast masses of land across the Atlantic Ocean to the west. They had made voyages of exploration prior to Columbus's discovery of the Antilles in 1492. But they had kept this knowledge to themselves, safeguarding it from their larger maritime rivals—Spain, England, and France.

Whatever the reasons, and no matter what landfall Cabral thought he had reached, he would have been astounded to know the immensity of the territory that lay beyond Brazil's rich coast, with its magnificent beaches and waving palms.

One of the strangest historical facts on record is that the ownership of Brazil had been established *before the land was even discovered!* This phenomenon came about because Spain and Portugal had become increasingly hostile over territorial claims as

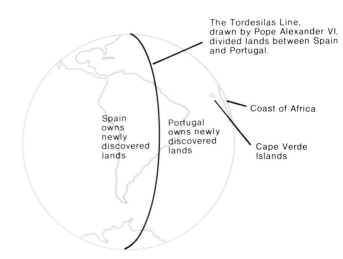

The Tordesilas Line, drawn by Pope Alexander VI, divided lands between Spain and Portugal.

Coast of Africa

Spain owns newly discovered lands

Portugal owns newly discovered lands

Cape Verde Islands

Portuguese explorer and navigator Pedro Álvares Cabral

each sent its most daring and skillful navigators on voyages of exploration and discovery. Pope Alexander VI, hoping to maintain peace between the two predominantly Catholic nations, drew up the Treaty of Tordesilas in 1494. This treaty, which both Spain and Portugal agreed to, established an imaginary dividing meridian, called the Tordesilas Line. It ran north to south from pole to pole and 370 leagues (about 1,500 miles) west of the Cape Verde Islands. All newly discovered lands east of the line would belong to Portugal; those to the west would belong to Spain.

Since the imaginary line ran from north to south almost through the center of what would later be Brazil, the country might have ended up half Portuguese and half Spanish. However, eighty years after Cabral's discovery and long before the interior of the land had been mapped, the thrones of the two countries were linked together under the Spanish crown and all of South America became a Spanish possession.

Motivated by Cabral's descriptions of a land that was a virtual paradise on earth, other Portuguese expeditions sailed to this new territory. Hoping to find gold, they had to be satisfied with a much lesser commodity, the red brazilwood that turned out to be readily marketable in Europe for making dyes and paints. Still, the potential for wealth and the appeal of the land as a Portuguese colony stimulated the imagination of Portugal's rulers. Official occupation began in 1530, when the first colonists were shipped to this new world with plentiful supplies of plants, seeds, and domestic animals. Ordered to establish permanent settlements to replace the original encampments, in 1532 the pioneers expanded São Vicente, located on the coast just south of what is now São Paulo.

Seventeen years later, Salvador became the official seat of the governor general. Located about halfway up the Atlantic coast in what is now the state of Bahia, this settlement was later to become one of the principal ports for the lucrative sugar industry, as well as a wealthy resort town. The Portuguese crown created a number of hereditary fiefs, or captaincies, along wide stretches of coastline, each governed by men who had already demonstrated their skills and leadership. Ironically, some of these private kingdoms were larger in size than Portugal itself.

THE COLONIAL PERIOD

Colonization became an established fact with the development of large sugar plantations along the northeast coast. Not only was the soil fertile for sugar, but Brazil was a natural point of call for ships following trade routes from Portugal to West Africa, South America, and the Orient. Europe was such an eager market for sugar that the colonists had to import slaves from West Africa to work the plantations. Particularly strong relations were established with the Dutch, prime marketers of sugar in Europe.

Two years after King Sebastian of Portugal died in 1578, Philip II of Spain successfully claimed the vacant Portuguese throne, uniting the two countries. This eliminated all disputes between Spain and Portugal over boundaries in South America. The Tordesilas Line, for example, no longer held any real meaning as a boundary that could divide Brazil in half.

When the Portuguese recovered their independence, in 1640 under John IV, their colonists in Brazil claimed all the territory they were occupying, even though much of it was by then in regions west of the original Tordesilas Line. Since Spain did not contest this claim—at least not with any vigor—Brazil, still largely a Portuguese territory, was able to keep all of its western boundaries, right up to the borders of Venezuela, Colombia, Peru, Bolivia, Paraguay, and Argentina.

The Brazilians had more of a problem with the Dutch at this time than with the Spanish. Using as an excuse the Thirty Years' War, a very complex war that involved many countries in Europe, the Dutch sent naval vessels to Brazil and seized many plantations, particularly in the state of Pernambuco. Although they held the sugar belt only from 1630 until they were ousted by the colonists in 1654, the Dutch influence can be seen in local architecture, family names, and some of the traditions.

A NEW GENERATION OF PIONEERS

Brazil might have continued for decades, even generations, as a coastal colony, limited in size and interests. But in the latter part of the seventeenth century, the demand for sugar began to decline. Feeling the economic pinch and lured by tales of gold and other riches in the interior, the planters and other colonists began

Gold was discovered near Ouro Preto in the 1690s.

forming groups to explore to the west and the southwest. They became known as the *bandeirantes* (flag bearers) as they headed into unknown territory, seeking gold, precious stones, and Indian slaves. Many of these frontiersmen, who took their own livestock, food plants, and seeds with them, were rough and relentless. But others were true pioneers, who played important roles in establishing new communities.

One of the important consequences of this pioneering movement was the discovery of gold in the 1690s near the present-day city of Ouro Preto (Black Gold). This discovery also led to the growth of Rio de Janeiro as a major city. Rio, located about 200 miles (322 kilometers) south of the goldfields, became the port through which the gold was shipped during the 1700s.

Gold quickly became the major source of wealth of Brazil and remained so during the entire eighteenth century. At first it was mined chiefly in the state of Minas Gerais, but later also in the states of Mato Grosso and Goiás.

An outgrowth of the gold boom was the birth and growth of the cattle industry. Because of the need for meat for the growing population in the interior and the need for leather for the mining of the ore, the cattle industry flourished.

The importation of coffee plants from French Guiana in the eighteenth century started another economic boom. It took many decades, however, before coffee came into its own about the middle of the nineteenth century. The first major plantations were in the southern part of the state of Rio de Janeiro. Later others appeared in the state of São Paulo.

Another key event in the second half of the eighteenth century was the transfer of the seat of government from Salvador to Rio. Again, gold was a motivating factor, since Rio dominated the access routes to the goldfields and was much closer than Salvador to the growing population centers of Brazil.

BRAZILIAN INDEPENDENCE

Brazil achieved its independence because of a historical circumstance. Late in the 1700s, a group of Brazilians, inspired by the ideals of the French Revolution and the American War of Independence, revolted against the Portuguese crown. The revolt, called the Minas Conspiracy, failed. But in 1808, the Portuguese royal family and a large group of nobles fled to Brazil when Portugal was threatened with invasion by Napoleon. Brazil became the seat of the Portuguese Empire.

Prince John (later King John VI) introduced a number of progressive measures. He removed most of the colonial

Dom Pedro II,
emperor of Brazil

restrictions on commerce and industry. He founded schools,
hospitals, a national library, and other important institutions.
These reforms ultimately led to the formation, in 1815, of the
United Kingdom of Brazil and Portugal, making Brazil coequal
with Portugal. It was then but a short step to real political
independence.

Six years later, the royal family returned to Portugal, with the
exception of one prince, Dom Pedro. On September 7, 1822, Dom
Pedro declared Brazil an independent empire. He assumed the
position of emperor as Dom Pedro I. Nine years later he turned
the leadership over to his son, Dom Pedro II, who was to hold that
office for fifty years.

Pedro II was known as a stern but temperate monarch. He ruled
the country more like a judge than an emperor and brought unity
and order to the nation. Brazil attained a new political and
cultural maturity. It reached a position of great stability internally,
as well as in international trade. Brazil became one of the best-
governed nations in the Western Hemisphere, with an

Slaves worked on Brazilian plantations.

administration that was totally honest and took prompt action against all kinds of abuses. Slavery was progressively eliminated over a period of years until, in 1888, complete abolition was suddenly declared. New health and welfare plans were instituted that were far ahead of their time. The educational system was greatly improved. Commerce and industry, agriculture, and transportation developed rapidly during this period.

Although internal peace brought harmony to all the peoples within the nation, Brazil was involved in three foreign wars—largely to protect itself from the threats of its neighbors. The first conflict was a short one against the Argentine tyrant Juan Manuel de Rosas in 1851-1852. The second one, from 1864 to 1870, saw the Brazilians battling the Uruguayans to the south, after troops from Uruguay began raids into the southern tip of Brazil to seize lands and goods. The third war, also from 1864 to 1870, repelled repeated invasions by Paraguay to the west, under the leadership of the Paraguayan dictator, Francisco Solano López.

It was characteristic of the Brazilians that, when they defeated their border enemies, they signed peace treaties without making demands for new territory. The borders stood as they had before. Brazil settled these conflicts by refusing to make claims for war debts or to ask to be reimbursed for the huge costs involved in protecting its territories. This attitude and spirit have become traditional and have been a factor in strengthening relationships with all of the countries that have common borders with Brazil.

THE REPUBLIC

Despite the many good works achieved by Pedro II and the honest and efficient administration of his government, there was a growing dissatisfaction with his leadership by the 1880s. One of the immediate causes of dissension was the emperor's abolition of slavery. While many Brazilians acknowledged that slavery was not in keeping with their Christian principles, they also felt that change had to come gradually in order to prevent a serious economic upheaval. As it was, complete abolition came so suddenly that it brought immense losses, and even ruin, to many of the landowners and the great plantations.

Dom Pedro was overthrown in November 1889 in a bloodless uprising and was banished to Portugal. Thus began a period that was to last until 1930, known as the First (or Old) Republic. It was characterized by rapid industrial progress and internal growth. In the transition from empire to republic, very few radical changes took place. The new order, although somewhat more liberal, followed the same broad pattern of the old regime. One of the basic changes was the subdivision of the country into states instead of provinces. Another was the introduction of an electoral system tor selecting presidents, the first of whom was Manuel Deodoro da Fonseca, one of the leaders of the revolt.

A constitution was drafted and adopted in 1891. It provided for a representative federal government, called the Republic of the United States of Brazil, and included a liberal bill of rights. Like the United States of America, the federal government authorized the individual states to adopt constitutions of their own.

The first few years saw a period of unrest as the various leaders of the country tried to solve some of the country's governmental and financial problems. But by 1894, Brazil had become stabilized both politically and economically, paving the way for an orderly succession of presidents and administrations for more than thirty-five years.

The First Republic continued until 1930 when, for the first time since its formation, the government was overthrown by force. The leader of the revolution, who then assumed power for the next fifteen years as head of state, was Getúlio Vargas. He based his revolt on growing dissatisfaction with the existing administration and the assertion that the president and his party had violated the rules of the electoral system in order to capture more votes.

Vargas took over the leadership of Brazil during troubled times. The Great Depression was affecting Brazil, as well as the rest of the world, and was responsible for a sharp decline in coffee prices. There was also a great deal of internal political strife, triggered by small groups of pro-Fascists and pro-Communists, who were influenced by the growing movements in Germany and Russia, respectively. Vargas at first attempted to establish a form of democracy under a revised constitution. When he failed to achieve unity, he declared a state of emergency, dissolved Congress, and assumed extraordinary powers to govern under an authoritarian charter. He became a dictator.

Citizens of Rio de Janeiro welcome the rebel troops led by General Getúlio Vargas in 1930.

Although the dictatorial rule of Vargas was criticized both at home and abroad, many of his accomplishments strengthened Brazil. By changing the constitution in the late 1930s, he formed the Estado Novo (New State), which in effect centralized the government and forced the development of industries and the diversification of agriculture throughout the country. Brazil worked its way out of the depression and into a state of strong economic stability prior to World War II.

The Vargas administration also reflected a new consciousness of nationality among Brazilians. This was a period that saw great public pride in cultural achievements, spearheaded by the paintings of Cândido Portinari, the architecture of Oscar Niemeyer and his Brazilian colleagues, and the music of Heitor Villa-Lobos. Vargas saw to it, too, that Brazil received recognition abroad by commissioning this kind of talent for the Brazilian Pavilion and exhibits at the New York World's Fair in 1939.

WORLD WAR II AND AFTERMATH

Brazil joined the Allies in 1942 and sent troops to Italy, where they fought with distinction against the Axis. Its great rubber

In February, 1943
President Getúlio Vargas
of Brazil (left) met with
President Franklin D. Roosevelt
of the United States to
discuss submarine warfare.
The Allies needed
Brazil's raw materials.

plantations along the Amazon and its ore mines provided badly
needed supplies for the Allied cause. And Brazil enhanced its
reputation in the Americas through a strengthening leadership in
inter-American affairs.

By the end of World War II, however, the Vargas regime fell
into decline and Vargas himself was ousted by a group of army
officers. Although he returned to power briefly in 1950, Vargas
was accused of mismanagement and was pressured to resign. He
committed suicide four years later.

The presidency since that time has been held largely by military
leaders, who have suppressed opposition parties and imposed
censorship in many cases. One of the significant regimes of
modern times was that of Juscelino Kubitschek, whose most
notable achievement was the planning and building of Brasília,
deep in the central highlands.

One of the most modern cities in the world, Brazil's new capital
was inaugurated in 1960 and has been acclaimed as a masterpiece
of architectural design and construction. Kubitschek also was
responsible for an ambitious program of highway and dam
construction and other engineering feats in a land where the
challenges of nature are many and awesome.

Bust of Juscelino Kubitschek, the man who made the dream of Brasília a reality

In the mid-1960s, after considerable economic, social, and political unrest, a new governmental structure was instituted by the military forces. It resulted in marked improvement in economic growth and industrial development, though not without some cost in political and social terms.

The federal constitution, which was approved in 1988, provides that the country shall be headed by a president and vice-president who are directly elected by the people for one five-year term. They are not immediately eligible for a second term. Voting is voluntary from the age of sixteen but compulsory between the ages of eighteen and seventy, and optional for those over seventy or illiterate. The new constitution eliminated censorship and the National Security Law.

Brazil's legislative authority is vested in the bicameral *Congreso Nacional*, Congress consists of an 81-member Senate (three senators per state) and a 503-member Chamber of Deputies. The Senate is two-thirds directly elected and one-third indirectly, for eight-year terms. The Chamber of Deputies is elected by universal franchise for four years.

According to the new constitution, Brazil is a union of 26 states, each with a directly elected governor and legislature, and a Federal District of Brazilia. The states and territories are divided into municipalities, which in turn are divided into districts.

View from Sugar Loaf. The Copa Beach is at left, Red Beach is
in the foreground, and Botatogo Bay is at right. The beach at
Ipanema (below) is always crowded.

Chapter 4

FAR-FLUNG CITIES
AND TOWNS

Ask a dozen foreigners what Brazilian city they think of first, and at least ten will probably answer, "Rio de Janeiro." The reasons for Rio's popularity are many. Its natural formations have made it more appealing than just about any other major city in the Americas. But Rio has far more than natural beauty.

Rio is Brazil's most important tourist center, not only for the many attractions it offers but for its position as a gateway to the other regions. With São Paulo, it forms the backbone of the southeast region. Historically, Rio was the nation's capital from 1763 until 1960, when Brasília became the official capital. Rio can justifiably be considered the cultural heart of Brazil. It has some of the nation's most distinguished centers, such as the National Museum of Fine Arts, the National Historical Museum, and the National Museum with more than a million exhibits relating to archaeology, zoology, ethnology, botany, and other sciences. Another internationally famous institution is the Botanical Garden, which was created in 1808. Drawing from the endless natural resources that lie within the sprawling boundaries of Brazil, as well as from lands abroad, the garden offers more than seven thousand varieties of plants.

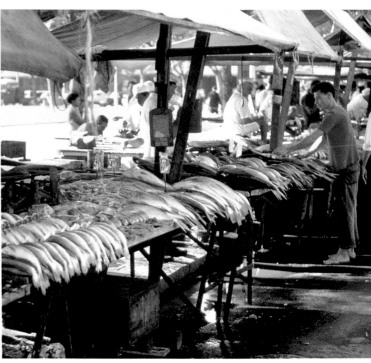

These narrow, crowded streets in Rio (top left) are for pedestrians only. The open-air fish market (top right), historic buildings at Lago do Boticário, (below left), and outdoor cafes (right) attract tourists.

Carnival parade (left) and Sugar Loaf Mountain (right)

The people of Rio are known as the *cariocas*. They have a worldwide reputation as friendly, charming, cosmopolitan folk, with rhythm in their movements and humor in their speech. The term *carioca* actually relates more to personal spirit and nature than to geographic origin.

There is immense interest in sports such as soccer, in dancing (especially the samba), and in various festivals and holidays. The greatest of all such events is the annual pre-Lenten carnival, with its riotous colors, imaginative floats, and endless music over a period of three days.

Rio is also a jewelry, fashion, and art center, exhibiting the works of many famous artists from all over the world in its galleries. It is a city of many hotels and restaurants, theaters, churches, samba schools, and public gardens. In short, it is ideal for residents and visitors alike as a place where there is always plenty to see and do, day and night, around the calendar.

Downtown São Paulo, Brazil

SÃO PAULO

São Paulo and Rio are often spoken of in the same breath. They are near neighbors in the southeast region and the two most important cities in Brazil, from the standpoint of international recognition and their importance to the nation's economy. Yet the two are leagues apart in character, as well as looks. Rio has been described as a city where people go to play and to spend money and São Paulo as the place where they go to work and to make money.

São Paulo, with a bustling population of more than nine million, is one of the oldest communities in the country. It was founded in 1554, barely half a century after Brazil was discovered, but did not come into its own until quite recently. The coffee boom gave the little town its first economic boost late in the

44

Metropolitan Cathedral (left). In São Paulo pedestrians use overpasses to cross busy streets.

nineteenth century. Yet even in the early 1900s, it was still a small, elegant old city with handsome gardens and somber public buildings. Then, in the 1920s, São Paulo began to show strong signs of industrial growth. By the 1930s it had overtaken Rio as the most important commercial center in the country. And by the 1960s, it was eclipsing Rio in population and growing at a faster rate than any other city in South America.

In some respects, São Paulo resembles New York City, with skyscrapers outlining the skyline. Among its buildings are more than three thousand bank branches, one thousand other financial institutions, and five hundred hotels of all sizes. It is the headquarters for just about every major corporation in Brazil, most of them international in scope. As such, it is responsible for more than half of the nation's industrial production.

As befits a modern city, São Paulo has many important cultural institutions, such as the Museum of Contemporary Art, the

*Acupuncture sign (left) is written in Portuguese and Japanese in
Japanese section of São Paulo. The maned wolf at the São Paulo
Zoo (right) is native to Brazil.*

Museum of Modern Art, the São Paulo Museum of Art, and the
Museum of Sacred Art. Its zoo, considered one of the seven best in
the world, has animals roaming in natural habitats scattered
throughout an immense park. A unique attraction is the Butantã
Institute, which exhibits some forty thousand examples of four
hundred species of snakes and other poisonous animals, largely
from the jungles of the interior.

Some sectors of the city reflect the ethnic and cultural origins of
foreign members of the populace. For example, there is a Japanese
sector, where streets and many of the buildings have Japanese
names. Traces of early Dutch, Spanish, and German influences can
also be found, along with evidence of the influence of commerce
and industry from the United States.

BRASÍLIA

Brasília is the capital of the nation. It is the most modern city of its size in South America, or for that matter in the entire Western Hemisphere. And it was in the planning stage for more than a century and a half as the ideal seat of government for the largest nation on the continent.

Brasília's origins go back to the time when Brazil was still a Portuguese colony. The leaders of the period had long felt that the capital, Rio de Janeiro, was vulnerable to attack by enemy ships or pirate fleets roaming the Atlantic. For security reasons alone, it seemed logical to shift the capital to the interior, where it could be defended more easily against invading troops in the event of war.

Many who sought Brazil's independence from Portugal early in the nineteenth century made plans to move the capital to São João del Rey, in the Minas Gerais territory. There, it could be better protected against Portuguese forces who would inevitably arrive to reclaim Brazil in the event that independence were declared. But the present location and name did not appear in historical records until 1821, one year before independence was proclaimed. That year, the leading statesman of the era, José Bonifácio de Andrada e Silva, drafted a resolution. It read in part: "In the center of Brazil, between the headwaters of the rivers which flow into the Paraguay and Amazon rivers, will be founded the capital of this realm, with the name of Brasília. . . . "

The dream of such a capital persisted for well over a century. It was not until the mid-1950s that the dream became a reality. In 1956, President Juscelino Kubitschek, who became known as "the father of Brasília," promised to build the city. The first step was to hold a major competition for the city's master plan. Twenty-six

View of Brasília as seen
from TV tower (top),
exterior of the Ministry of
Justice (middle left),
Congress as seen from
the Presidential Palace
(middle right), and the
interior of the National
Cathedral (left)

architects competed. The winner was Lúcio Costa. In one of the most remarkable building feats of modern times, the center of Brasília was built in just three years, bringing together a dedicated team of designers, contractors, construction specialists, artists, and others. The immense labor force that converged on the region became known as the *candangos*, workers from every corner of the country.

Costa's design for the city layout was indeed unusual, resembling a jet plane with swept back wings. Two axis lines cross each other at right angles to connect north with south and east with west. As a result, sections of the city are referred to by such terms as North Wing and South Wing. The residential sections are in areas known as superblocks, clusters of six-story buildings, each completely self-sufficient, with all services needed by the occupants. Between these blocks lie parks, schools, commercial centers, and theaters.

The noted Brazilian architect Oscar Niemeyer designed the major buildings. The buildings are so light and airy that they seem to float in the air. Among the most noted structures are the *Palácio da Alvorada* (Palace of Dawn), *Praça dos Três Poderes* (Square of the Three Powers), and the Ministry of Foreign Affairs, a showplace with magnificent gardens, man-made lakes, and interior works of art. Also of great interest are the National Cathedral, designed in the shape of an inverted chalice, and the National Theater, which has three separate stages.

Brasília is particularly stunning at night, when the exteriors and interiors of the buildings are illuminated with modern and effective lighting equipment, specially designed for the purpose. Brasília, day or night, is like no other city in all of South America.

CITIES AND TOWNS OF THE INTERIOR

Brazil is unique in another way. No other country, not even in the heart of Africa, has so many important cities and towns hidden away in the frontiers and wildernesses. Manaus is a fine example.

Capital of the state of Amazonas and combining the old with the new, Manaus has been described as "a flower blossoming out of the jungle." The city is so deep in the interior that it takes from three to five days to reach it by boat from the coast, sailing up the Amazon from the Atlantic port of Belém. Almost since its founding in 1850, Manaus has enjoyed all the comforts of civilization, while surrounded by the largest and densest forests on earth. A little more than half an hour from Manaus by small boat are jungles that have been penetrated by very few people other than the native Indians.

Fascination with this region goes back to 1539, when a Spanish explorer, Francisco de Orellana, traveled up the mighty river and was almost killed in a battle with Indians. He described the enemy as female warriors, an allusion to the Amazons of Greek mythology, which is how the Amazon got its name. It was not until three hundred years later that a permanent camp was established in the region.

Manaus became something more than a jungle outpost when a demand for rubber arose. The trees from which latex is extracted to manufacture rubber grew in abundance in the Amazon region. Within a very few years, Manaus grew from a quiet wilderness village to a bustling city. The influx of great wealth from the rubber plantations resulted in a city designed along European lines. It was attractively laid out with parks, wide avenues, public

Manaus (left) is on the Rio Negro. Its Opera House (right) was built in 1910 with the money made from rubber.

squares—and even British-style bandstands. The wealthier inhabitants, desiring to live as comfortably as possible, financed a large waterworks, developed an efficient trash collection and disposal system, built trams for transportation, and even installed electric lights before the end of the nineteenth century.

Undaunted by time and distance, the developers of Manaus imported everything they wanted from Europe. The customs house, for example, was shipped, stone by stone, from Liverpool, England. Expensive marble from Italy was used to add elegance to buildings that also had items imported from Portugal, Spain, and France. Among its cultural institutions were a large public library, several theaters, museums, a botanical garden, and the world-famous *Teatro Amazonas* (Amazon Theater), which seated more than a thousand people and reputedly cost $2 million, a sum equal to about $40 million today. The wood used in its construction came from the nearby rain forest, but all other building materials were shipped from Europe.

Waterfront market on Rio Negro at Manaus (left). Cranes unload containers at the port.

The decline of the rubber boom was inevitable. It was hastened for the Amazon region when an Englishman named Wickman broke the Brazilian monopoly on latex by smuggling thousands of rubber tree cuttings to Malaysia, where they began to thrive. Within a few years, the price of Brazilian rubber plummeted about 50 percent, and the wealthy image of Manaus began to deteriorate. Today, the city is a tourist center and the gateway to the jungle interior. Its Old-World charm still exists in its buildings, its mosaic sidewalks, its broad tree-lined avenues, and its European-style squares, with their fountains. The city is often visited by travelers who want the comfortable adventure of seeing the jungles from excursion boats. But it is also the headquarters for bands of explorers and scientists heading for the uncharted interior, where real dangers still lurk on all sides.

JUNGLE OUTPOSTS

Travelers who venture past Manaus are advised not to swim in the waters of the Amazon or any other jungle rivers. Fish that normally live in salt water, like sharks and sawfish, may be found as far as 2,000 miles (3,218 kilometers) from the sea. They share the murky waters with electric eels, snakes, piranhas, and giant horned catfish that often weigh four hundred pounds (181 kilograms). Along the shores, jaguars and ocelots slink through the trees; giant armadillos come to the water to drink; and anteaters poke about the earth with their long, probing snouts.

In this northwestern region of Brazil, roads are almost nonexistent and transportation is either by riverboat or small plane. Astonishingly, there are more than fifty towns in the Amazon region, though few are ever visited by foreigners. Two such towns are Porto Velho, capital of the territory of Rondônia, and Rio Branco, capital of the state of Acre.

Porto Velho is one of the few places in Amazonia that can be reached by motor vehicles. The trip involves a two-day bus trip from Manaus, along some 550 miles (885 kilometers) of narrow, winding road that has been hacked through the jungles. The trip by boat is more comfortable and scenic, though it may take from four to seven days. At one time a railroad was contemplated, to cut through the forests to the west, all the way to the Bolivian Andes. Only a single station and the local Railroad Museum remain of this plan. In this case, nature triumphed.

Rio Branco lies 350 miles (563 kilometers) beyond Porto Velho, near the headwaters of the Purus River, which has yellow waters and has been called the forsaken river. This frontier town, with a population of over 400,000 people (about half the size of Porto

Ferry carries a bus and its passengers from Porto Velho.

Velho), almost straddles the Andean borders of Peru and Bolivia. Although Rio Branco is situated some 2,000 miles (3,218 kilometers) from any Atlantic coast port, it is still involved in the extraction and refinement of natural rubber.

One other important wilderness city is Cuiabá, capital of Mato Grosso. Mato Grosso is second only to the Amazon region as an area of great wildernesses and frontiers. Known as the Brazilian West, this was the last region of Brazil to be developed. Although settlements had been established near Cuiabá in the eighteenth century, when gold was discovered there, and though cattle had been introduced even earlier, "civilization" as such was still lacking. Many of these settlements either vanished from the face of the earth or were so isolated they were soon forgotten.

In rural Brazil small villages are common.

Until the advent of the airplane, it took many weeks to reach Cuiabá. One had to travel by railroad to the end of the line at the Paraguay River and then by boat. The region is still so remote that, although the states of Mato Grosso and neighboring Gojás account for almost a quarter of the total territory of Brazil, it has just over 4 percent of the population.

Much of the development of Cuiabá occurred in the 1930s, when then President Getúlio Vargas publicized a slogan, *Marcha para o Oeste* (March to the West). His idea was to enlarge and improve western communities in the hope that more gold and other precious metals would be mined, thus improving the country's economy. In 1933, he even built a brand new city, Goiana, as the new, progressive capital of the state of Goiás.

Cuiabá is also the northern gateway to the great Pantanal marshlands, one of the last great ecological preserves in the Americas, and the home of thousands of species of animals, birds, fish, and plants. Cuiabá attracts naturalists and other nature lovers, who can find convenient transportation into the Pantanal or to other wild environments nearby, to observe nature at its rarest and finest.

Old section of Belém

BELÉM: GATEWAY TO THE NORTH

Because of its position at the wide mouth of the Amazon River, Belém is the nearest gateway to Brazil from the United States. Situated on the Atlantic coast at the top of Brazil, its port teems with ships of all kinds and sizes—some oceangoing and many designed mainly for river travel to the west.

Characteristic of this old city, founded in 1616, is the Ver-o-Peso (See the Weight) Market. The name comes from the fact that, during colonial times, officials of the crown were stationed at the market to "see the weight" and set the amounts of taxes to be charged. This colorful waterfront attraction with its old stalls and archways was designed and constructed in England and then transported to Brazil. Every day, starting at 6:00 A.M., vendors in boats and canoes bring local products and crafts to sell. These include endless varieties of tropical fruits, vegetables, fish, local handicrafts, medicinal herbs, and native artifacts.

Belém's boats (left) and market area can be seen from Fort Castelo

Many of the buildings in Belém are old, some dating from the seventeenth century. Among these are the baroque Mercês Church, oldest in the city, and the cathedral (1742), which contains valuable religious paintings and other works of art. One of the city's chief attractions is Fort Castelo, located at the point where the Guamá River, one of the many branches of the Amazon, joins Guajará Bay. The fort, which was the birthplace of the city, still has its bronze cannons, pointing seaward.

Just to the northwest of Belém, at the mouth of the Amazon River, lies huge Marajó Island. Almost twice the size of the state of Massachusetts, it is made up of low plains that are periodically flooded, forming hundreds of small islands. The island is the site of the Marajoara culture, one of the great pre-Columbian Indian civilizations in the Americas. There is a great deal of mystery about the history and origins of the Marajoaras, whose descendants may be seen today, dressed as their ancestors were centuries ago. Much of the pottery, for which they were noted, still exists, on display in the Emílio Goeldi Museum in Belém.

Old port and crowded market (left) and Ladeira do Pelourinho (right), in Salvador.

SALVADOR: ON THE GOLDEN COAST

Founded in 1549, Salvador was the first capital of Brazil, a status it held until 1763. Sometimes called Bahia, because it is the capital of the state of Bahia, the city has two distinct levels. The Lower City, at sea level, contains the old port and commerical district, where much of the region's merchandise is still peddled. Sales of products—from arts and crafts, carvings, and silver, to native fruits, homemade sweets, and straw objects—are accompanied by singing and dancing. This district is also the scene of much entertainment, including the *capoeira*, a combination of jujitsu and the dance. It was originally a form of lethal combat that has, fortunately, been modified into a style of folk dance.

The Upper City is reached by stone steps, alleyways, and the Lacerda elevator, all of which rise 234 feet (71 meters) from the lower level. This part of the city contains the government buildings, museums, churches, and the main residential districts.

Salvador, sometimes called "the land of all saints," is also a city

This unusual elevator (left) travels from lower part of Salvador to the upper part. Church of São Francisco is one of the city's many churches.

of churches. According to one samba song, Bahia has 365 churches—one for each day of the year. Although this is an exaggeration, it is true that the city has hundreds of churches. Many of them are elegant and ancient. Typical examples are the Church of São Francisco de Assis, erected in 1581, with a magnificent carved gold-leaf altar; the Aflitos Church, dating from the seventeenth century; and the Church of Grace, built in 1577.

Side by side with the Catholic religion is a form of African rite known as *Candomblé*. This complex ritual, based on religious practices of West Africa, was brought to Brazil by the early slaves. Modern day *Candomblé* includes some Portuguese Catholic traditions, and it is common for practitioners of these mystic rites to attend Mass on Sundays.

Salvador, a center for artists, writers, sculptors, and musicians, has played an important part in the culture of Brazil for more than a century.

Vendors on the beach of Recife

RECIFE: THE VENICE OF BRAZIL

As the second largest city of the northeastern region, Recife has more than 1.4 million inhabitants and is a major center of commerce and industry. This capital of the state of Pernambuco started as a tiny colony of fishermen in the sixteenth century and rose to importance after the Dutch invasion of the region in 1630. Its name derives from the *arrecifes* (reefs) that protect its sheltered harbor. Its nickname is the Venice of Brazil. It was built on the delta of the Capibaribe and Beberibe rivers, which had many channels crisscrossing the land. Over the years, these were modified and dredged so that they formed a network of small canals. Like the Italian city of Venice, Recife is dotted with innumerable bridges of varying sizes, which carry vehicular and foot traffic across the waterways.

Recife thrived commercially as a major port for the exportation of cotton to other parts of Brazil and the world. Today it is an industrial center that produces textiles, foods, chemicals, electrical appliances, communications equipment, and engineering facilities. Much of the architectural legacy of the early Dutch settlers is still preserved, along with that of more recent groups of Europeans and Brazilians who have migrated to this coastal city.

THE HIGHLAND AND MOUNTAIN CITIES

Brazil has relatively few regions that could be described as mountainous in comparison with other countries along the western rim of the South American Andes. But its highland areas are quite different from the lowlands. The Eastern Highlands include most of the state of Minas Gerais, located directly north of Rio de Janeiro and southwest of the coastal cities described earlier. It consists mainly of hilly uplands that are generally at an altitude of between 2,500 and 2,800 feet (762 and 853 meters). But it also includes the Serra do Espinhaço, a mountain range that reaches up to 4,200 feet (1,280 meters).

The settlement of this highland region really began during the gold boom in the seventeenth century. In 1698, gold had been discovered by an expedition of *bandeirantes* from São Paulo. The *bandeirantes* were so named because they carried flags (*bandeiras*) bearing their family coats of arms. Blazing trails through the forests, these pioneers established small settlements at the sites where they discovered gold and, later, diamonds and other precious stones. Some of these settlements thrived and became towns and cities. One was Ouro Preto.

OURO PRETO

Originally named Vila Rica (Rich Town), Ouro Preto (Black Gold) derived its name from the discoveries made there. Once the richest mining town in Brazil, the city's gold boom lasted almost one hundred years. Ouro Preto reflects the opulence of that era and the tremendous influence that gold and other precious metals and gems had on Brazilian history and on the country's

Belo Horizonte (left) and the Church of San Francisco in Ouro Preto (right)

international economy. In the mid-eighteenth century, the city acquired a rich elegance that, fortunately, has been preserved to the present day. The city is, in fact, such a rarity that in 1980 it was declared by UNESCO to be "a cultural monument for all mankind." It is now referred to by Brazilians as their National Monument City.

Much of the city's splendor was created by a genius of the day, the sculptor Antônio Francisco Lisboa. Known as "The Little Cripple," he was so handicapped by arthritis and leprosy that he had to work with tools strapped to his hands. He created vast numbers of magnificent carvings of wood and stone, which exist today in the architecture of the region. One of his greatest works of art depicts the Apostles and sixty-six other figures that tell the story of Christ from the Last Supper to the Crucifixion. A fellow artist, João Ataide, painted wondrous murals and ceilings in the churches for which the sculptor did the carvings.

Ouro Preto is one of the highest cities in Brazil, at an altitude of about 3,500 feet (1,067 meters), with a climate that is temperate and pleasant. The city attracts not only tourists, but also historians, architects, sculptors, painters, composers, and other professionals from all over the world, who find it a living monument to art and culture. Ouro Preto's museums are internationally famous. Some exhibit works of art, others are historical in nature. The Mineralogy Museum is one of the largest of its kind in the Western Hemisphere, housing precious gems, examples of the city's black gold, and intricate rock crystals.

The small town of Congonhas, about 45 miles (72 kilometers) from Ouro Preto, enjoys a unique distinction. Because Antônio Francisco Lisboa lived and worked here, it houses his largest work—the twelve prophets, carved in soapstone and standing in the churchyard of the Basílica de Bom Jesus de Matozinhos. During Holy Week, main areas of the town are transformed into scenes from the Bible. Almost the entire population takes part in staging the main events of the life of Jesus Christ.

BELO HORIZONTE

The Eastern Highland area is characterized by many small hill towns with populations of less than five thousand. But it is also the site of the third largest city in Brazil, Belo Horizonte (Beautiful Horizon), with a population nearing three million. The city, capital of the state of Minas Gerais, spreads out along a plateau that rises about 2,700 feet (823 meters) above sea level. Tourists know it as the gateway to surrounding towns rich in history and art. Business executives think of it in different terms— as the home of auto plants, steel mills, and other heavy industry and as the center of rich iron-ore deposits that cover more than 100,000 square miles (259,000 square kilometers).

Not far from Belo Horizonte are the impressive grottos of Lapinha and Maquiné. Both caverns contain great underground halls, some as much as 50 feet (15 meters) in height, along with an intricate network of galleries and labyrinths, with stalactites, stalagmites, and extensive limestone crystal formations.

The origins of Belo Horizonte are much more recent than those of the old colonial towns. It was in 1893 that the government of the state of Minas Gerais decided that the existing capital, Ouro Preto, was not environmentally suited to greater expansion. Thus, the new city was planned. The streets intersect each other at right angles and are crossed diagonally by avenues lying at 45-degree angles to the streets, just like those of Washington, D.C. At the time of its inauguration in 1897, the new city had a population of only ten thousand and growth was much slower than planned. But by the 1930s rapid industrial development accelerated this growth. Today the city and its suburbs sprawl over many square miles.

CITIES OF THE SOUTHERN COUNTRYSIDE

The southernmost states of Brazil are the coolest and most temperate. That is because Brazil lies below the equator, where the climate is reversed from the climate found above the equator.

The city of Porto Alegre, capital of the state of Rio Grande do Sul, ranks as one of the most important commercial centers in Brazil. It is one of the few melting pots in the country, with a mixture of native Brazilians, Portuguese, Italians, Germans, and other European stock. Although the city was founded in 1740, it continued for a century or more to be rural in nature. It was chiefly a market and center of activity for the cattle raising that

*Crowded streets
of Porto Alegre*

Brasília

Belo
Horizonte

Curitiba

Ouro Prêto

Rio de Janeiro

Florianópolis

Pôrto Alegre

prospered in the low hills and valleys that surround the city and
the Guaíba River.

All that changed when colonists from Europe arrived during
the nineteenth century and started small manufacturing
operations. Within a single generation, they were producing
fabrics, shoes, metals, many kinds of foods, vehicles, clothing, and
wines. The Europeans also established many restaurants, serving
traditional dishes from Italy, Germany, Spain, and Portugal, along
with local wines produced from grape plantings brought from the
other side of the Atlantic. In the matter of food, though, they had
to compete with what was then—and still is—a great favorite,
churrasco, created by the *gaúchos* of the southern plains. *Churrasco*
is meat broiled over glowing coals, then cut into chunks and
seasoned carefully with salt. It is usually served with *chimarrão,* a
bitter herb tea served hot in gourds.

North of Porto Alegre is the city of Florianópolis, partly situated
on an Atlantic island, Santa Catarina, from which it is connected
to the mainland by two bridges. One of these, the Hercílio Luz, is
the largest steel suspension bridge in Brazil.

The capital of the state of Santa Catarina, Florianópolis is in
effect two cities. The island portion, with narrow streets and

Florianópolis

stately mansions, represents the older city, which began as a
coastal settlement in the 1670s. It was later populated by
immigrants from the Azore Islands, and for a short while, invaded
by Spaniards. Because of its island location, it long remained
isolated and little developed.

The mainland section of Florianópolis is quite another world,
bustling with activity and heavy with traffic. There the city is the
center of government administration and industrial development.
A third sector of the economy, which affects both parts of the city,
is tourism. People come to tour the historic buildings and
museums, as well as to enjoy the many glorious stretches of
beach.

Among the other important communities of Brazil's southern
region are Curitiba, capital of the state of Paraná, which has a
mixed ethnic background of German, Italian, and Polish;
Paranaguá, which can be approached by train along a series of
dramatic precipices and is a major coffee exporting port; Caxias
do Sul, center of the largest wine producing region in Brazil; and
Iguaçu, situated where the borders of Brazil, Argentina, and
Paraguay meet, and the location of the famous falls that have been
compared with Niagara in terms of their might and splendor.

Rio coastline from Corcovado

Brazil's cities and towns reflect the revolutionary changes that have taken place in the nation within recent times. In less than fifty years, Brazil had been transformed from a rural society into an urban one. Just before World War II, only 30 percent of the population lived in the cities. By 1980, that figure had climbed to well over 60 percent. Government estimates that predicted the next decade would see less than 30 percent of the people in rural areas and over 70 percent in the cities proved true.

This dramatic increase can be accounted for partly by the natural growth in the urban population and partly by an influx of immigrants, who usually choose to settle in the cities and larger towns. But the most significant factor has been the migration of Brazilians from the traditionally poorer countryside to the urban locations, where the pay is higher and the job opportunities greater. Another factor, generally overlooked, is that Brazil is a nation of young people. As stated earlier, at least 35 percent of the population is under fifteen years of age. Young people tend to head for the cities if they live in rural areas and small towns. If they are already in urban areas, they stay there.

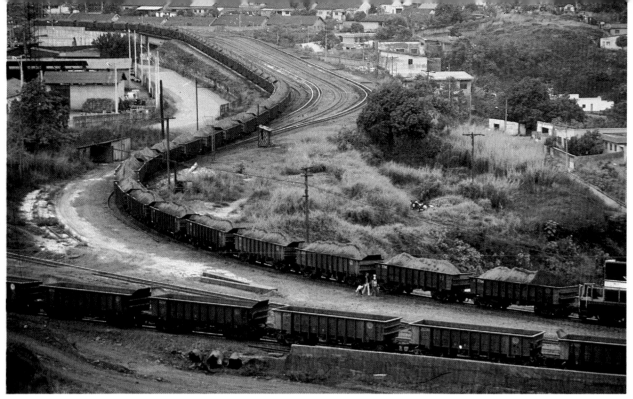

Freight trains (above) carry iron ore, the most important
mineral product exported by Brazil, from the mine at Itabira.
Hydroelectric installations at Paulo Afonso Falls (below)
supply power to seven states from Ceará to Bahia.

Chapter 5

A MULTIFACETED ECONOMY

In recent times, with the Brazilian economy stifled by
recessions, inflation, and unemployment, one economist joked,
"That's nothing new. Brazil started out in the red." Of course, he
referred to the first exploitable product of the earliest colonists—
the red dye extracted from brazilwood that gave the country its
name. The demand for this resource led to the establishment of
the first European settlements in Brazil—three trading posts at
Recife, São Vicente, and Piratininga in 1502, barely two years after
the coast was discovered.

Today, Brazil's economy is still based mainly on the land's
natural resources and agriculture, despite intensive concentration
on industrial development. Brazil is very rich in natural resources.
In addition to having some of the largest iron ore deposits in the
world, the land yields increasing amounts of other metals,
minerals, and precious stones. Vast amounts of potential power
are available through extensive waterways, which are being
harnessed as hydroelectric systems. Although major deposits of
oil and gas have yet to be discovered, there is great promise that
such discoveries will be made, perhaps in interior regions that
have been little explored and almost totally unexploited.

The country's major industries include steel production,

shipbuilding, vehicle manufacture, and petrochemicals. Since the health of the economy hinges on increasing exports and reducing imports, the development of natural resources and agriculture holds the most promise for the immediate and long-range future. Before looking ahead, though, it is necessary to evaluate the past.

HISTORICAL EVOLUTION OF THE BRAZILIAN ECONOMY

Brazil's colonization by the Portuguese was in itself a commercial enterprise. Since Portugal was a small country whose trade was often stifled by her much larger competitors in Europe—especially Spain, England, and France—she badly needed Brazil's huge, untapped resources.

The real business of profitable colonization started with the sugar plantations of the northeast, along the Atlantic, at the end of the sixteenth century. Portugal's dominance as a seagoing nation, with some of the finest ships and navigators in the world, made two things possible. The first was the importation to Brazil of slave labor from West Africa, rapidly improving the growth and output of the plantations. The second was the capability of shipping sugar efficiently to the best markets in Europe and then turning the ships around with new groups of settlers and cargoes of supplies for the New World.

Brazil's economy was devastated when the West Indies began to capture the sugar market in Europe. The plantations in the Pernambuco region fell into a steady decline. By the end of the century, though, Brazil had a new lease on life when the *bandeirantes* discovered gold in the Eastern Highlands in what is now the state of Minas Gerais. The economic center of the country shifted from the northeast, and with it much of the slave labor. Rio de Janeiro began to flourish as the new capital of the country and the port from which most of the gold was shipped.

The government was still too inexperienced in matters of economy to have learned a lesson from the sugar failure. Thus when the gold boom ended, the nation had no other exports to fall back on. The sugar market was still poor. Cotton, which at one time had seemed promising, had not been developed enough to compete with the cotton from North American plantations. The same was true of other crops, including tobacco, cocoa, and rice. Nor had the cattle industry yet perfected the production of hides.

One other factor hurt the economy. Instead of encouraging Brazil to build manufacturing facilities during colonial days, Portugal had considered its new colony as a market for its own products. Thus, Brazil was saddled early in its history with having to import more than it exported. Even after Brazil achieved independence, she had to sign a trade agreement with England, once Portugal's close trading partner. According to the agreement, England could export manufactured goods to Brazil at low tariff rates. Brazil had so little to export to England, in turn, that the agreement was more of a disadvantage than an advantage. It was not until 1844, when the treaty lapsed, that Brazil was able to increase import duties and profit from increased revenues.

In the middle of the nineteenth century, the largest and potentially the greatest nation in South America was as financially distressed as its poorest neighbors. Brazil desperately needed to produce great quantities of some kind of export commodity that would be in demand in the free markets of the world. Ironically, it had been growing the ideal export crop for generations.

Agricultural inspector examines coffee beans. Coffee is one of Brazil's major exports.

THE RICHNESS OF COFFEE

Coffee had been produced as a crop in Brazil in the early eighteenth century, when seeds and seedlings were brought into what is now the northern state of Pará in 1727 from neighboring French Guiana. From Pará, coffee plants were sent to a number of other locations, including Rio, where they were grown as a kitchen garden crop. By 1810, coffee plantations had been established throughout the province of Rio de Janeiro and were beginning to produce in considerable quantity. The coffee tree flourished in the climate and soil of Brazil, particularly in the south-central area of the country, where there was high ground and regular rainfall.

After getting off to a slow start, coffee became Brazil's most important crop. By 1870, Brazil was producing about half of the world's supply. Coffee was putting the country back on its feet again economically. The cultivation of coffee was encouraged by a number of factors, including the foreign demand and the lifting of trade restrictions. Also, because of the decline in mining, there was more money available within the country for investment in coffee. Cultivation and harvesting costs were relatively low. In addition, a brand-new market was emerging in the United States, where coffee was beginning to replace tea as the national drink.

The popularity of coffee and the wealth that it brought to Brazil produced a new class of landed gentry, the coffee barons. They were to be very influential in the affairs of Brazil, particularly in the sectors around Rio and São Paulo.

Thousands of acres that had once been thick forest and woodlands gave way to the coffee tree. But before long the soil became eroded. Too many trees had been felled; the soil lacked the nutrients and organic matter that had been provided by the forests. The result was a gradual movement of the coffee plantations, first onto the São Paulo plateau and then farther west.

Another major change took place after the abolition of slavery in 1888. It became difficult to find suitable labor forces for the fields. Even when workers were found, the cost of wages introduced a new financial problem. A partial solution was the importation of many thousands of foreign laborers, mainly from Italy. In 1895, the peak year of this wave of immigration, more than 140,000 laborers migrated to southern Brazil from Europe.

Coffee transformed the economy of Brazil, particularly in the southeast region, where most of the large plantations were located. Historically, this concentration of plantations was one of the reasons why the government of the country shifted from the northeast to the areas around Rio and São Paulo. Other developments followed, such as the construction of railway lines and roads near the plantations and the improvement of southern ports, to handle the export of coffee to worldwide markets. The coffee boom continued until 1930, when the Great Depression seriously limited all markets for commodities.

RUBBER: BOOM AND BUST

Although coffee dominated Brazil's economy in the nineteenth century, rubber made a brief appearance as a promising money-maker. Rubber had been used locally for a number of purposes, mainly in the Amazon region where the rubber trees grew wild. But draining the latex from the trees and putting it to any great commercial use was beyond the capabilities of those who tried to do so early in the nineteenth century.

The situation changed dramatically when an American inventor, Charles Goodyear, developed a method of treating rubber called vulcanization in 1839. The process made it possible to transform latex into rubber products that were strong, resilient, and elastic and that resisted heat, cold, and chemicals. Before the Goodyear process, Brazil had exported only a few hundred tons of rubber. But by 1850, it was exporting some 1,500 tons (1,364 metric tons). Before the end of the century, the annual exports totaled 30,000 tons (27,273 metric tons) and more.

At the height of the rubber boom, Brazil supplied half of the entire world production of rubber, all from the heart of the Amazon region. Unfortunately, only a small group of Brazilians profited from the exploitation of rubber. The so-called rubber kings became rich and spent their money extravagantly, building ornate mansions and traveling the world extensively. They designed and developed the city of Manaus on the Amazon River as a rich backdrop, importing just about every luxury that money could buy. At the same time, the laborers who went into the forests to tap the rubber trees and bring out pails of liquid latex lived in wretched poverty. They had to cope with the hardships of heat, humidity, and stinging insects and were exposed daily to the

Ripe cacao pods (left). Laborers load cotton into trucks for shipment to the textile mills.

dangers of wild animals, snakes, and marauding natives.

The boom collapsed when rubber trees were successfully planted in Malaysia, Indonesia, and Ceylon, undercutting the Brazilian market in price and making the product more easily accessible. Once more, the Brazilian economy faltered.

A TRY AT COCOA AND COTTON

Cocoa (*cacao* in Brazil), which is said to have originated in Aztec Mexico, was first grown commercially in Brazil more than two centuries ago. It had been imported from Amazonia to the southern Bahia region, along the Atlantic coast. There the climate and soil conditions were ideal for this tropical tree with its large pods of beans. Not until the middle of the nineteenth century, though, did cocoa have value for anything but local household use. One of the factors that hastened its commercialization was the importation of seedlings from Ceylon. These yielded more beans per tree and produced a high-quality cocoa. By 1910, thousands of acres of the new trees were supplying beans, just at a time when the chocolate industry in Europe was growing and there was a constant demand for cocoa.

The demand was so great during this era that many Brazilians in the southern Bahia region were engaged in buying, selling, and developing the kind of land that was particularly suited to this rich crop. Since lands were at a premium and limited in extent, the ensuing "Cocoa Rush" triggered a considerable amount of violence and bloodshed. At first the lands were cleared by small farmers from the northeast. These developed into plantations as the price of cocoa rose on the international market. Then business groups from the cities began investing in the lands, as well as speculating on cocoa in the stock market. More and more plantations passed from agricultural owners into the hands of urban businessmen and sometimes large corporations.

Like cocoa, cotton thrived in southern Bahia and had been planted there during colonial days. It, too, was of little importance commercially at first. It was grown by farmers and families primarily for personal use in the making of clothes and furnishings for the home. Although cotton became an export crop in the middle of the nineteenth century, it never flourished to such an extent that it caused a boom. At one time, however, it was Brazil's number two export.

Cotton had—and continues to have—one advantage over cocoa and some of the other Brazilian crops. It can be raised easily all over the country, except in the southern tip. For this reason, the raising of cotton gradually shifted from the northeast to the southeast, eventually making the state of São Paulo the area of greatest production.

CATTLE RAISING

Brazil has one of the largest herds of beef cattle in the world with over 145 million head. Cattle raising started in the northeast during colonial times, largely to supply meat for the sugar plantations. As the plantations grew, so did grazing fields nearby, where herds were controlled by gauchos, the name given South American cowboys. But when the sugar plantations declined, the cattle industry declined, too.

The situation was different in the south. When the coffee boom began in the states of São Paulo and Paraná, grazing lands were set aside for cattle, just as they had been in the northeast. The initial objective was simply to provide meat and hides for the owners of the coffee lands and their workers. Cattle had grazed the wide open *pampas* (plains) of the south for generations. Now landowners with foresight began raising cattle as commercial ventures, not just to feed themselves and their neighbors.

It was not long before the breeding of livestock began to spread throughout the rest of Brazil. Large ranches, known as *estâncias*, became commonplace. The cowboys, too, came into their own, many of them partly Indian and accustomed to riding herd all day long and living in the open. Their form of dress became distinctive, characterized by leather clothing as protection against the thorny growths of scrubby plants known as *caatinga*.

The state of Minas Gerais already had many pasturelands devoted to the raising of livestock. These animals supplied food for the mine owners and workers, whose ranks increased as new deposits of ore were discovered. One strain of cattle, known in South America as *zebu*, predominated. This breed was particularly resistant to ticks, parasites, and infection. Brought in from India,

Gaúchos guard herds of zebu, *a hardy strain of cattle developed to resist ticks, parasites, and infection.*

zebus were interbred with domestic Brazilian strains for livestock that produced more meat.

FISHING

Like any nation with a large seacoast, Brazil always has had fishing fleets. Until recent times, these were local in nature, bringing fish to nearby markets for sale the same day each catch was brought ashore. Curiously enough, Brazilians are not great fish eaters, despite the extent of their shoreline or the magnitude of their inland waters. Although fish is a staple up and down the Atlantic and gourmet dishes are available in fine restaurants, the inland populations tend to omit fish from their diets. This dietary habit began, of course, with the problems of keeping fish fresh in a warm climate. Yet the habit seems to have persisted in many regions, despite the availability of refrigeration.

*These fishing boats use their sails as billboards,
advertising a variety of products and services.*

Fishing along the Brazilian coast has always been an occupation
with more color and romance than economic value. In the
northeast, fishermen still head far out to sea in frail boats or on
rafts known as *jangadas*. Hence, they long ago became known as
jangadeiros, men of daring.

With all the fish available to them, the Portuguese who came to
Brazil could find none in the nearby Atlantic waters to suit their
tastes. They were accustomed to codfish, or *bacalhau*, caught off
the Newfoundland banks. Thus, one of their principal imports
became codfish, salted and dried, from the east coast of North
America!

In recent years, the Japanese in Brazil have become the most
active commercial fishermen, ranging far out to sea with their
trawlers in search of tuna and lobster. Fishing has become an
important industry in Brazil, particularly in the northeast and the
south. There is an abundance of fish and shellfish of high
commercial value off the northeastern coast. Large schools of
lower-grade fish are prolific off the southern coast. Millions of
cans of sardines are produced in Brazilian canneries. The other
major exports are lobsters and shrimp.

MINING AND MINERAL RESOURCES

Minas Gerais is still the hub of Brazilian gold mining, but exports have dwindled to a mere fraction of what they were in the nineteenth century. Today iron ore is the most important mineral product exported by Brazil. Minas Gerais is also the source of all commercial production of iron, which is shipped largely to Japan, Germany, and the United States.

Brazil has the world's largest reserves of iron ore, much of it 60 percent pure iron. It is estimated that more than sixty billion tons have not yet been touched. One enormous discovery, which was made in the early 1970s in the Carajós Mountains, could alone equal one third of all the iron reserves in Brazil.

Besides iron ore, Brazil produces large quantities of bauxite for the aluminum industry. The richest deposits to date have been located on the Trombetas River in the lower Amazon region and in the jungles of the wild state of Pará in north-central Brazil. Other important minerals are manganese, nickel, tin, tungsten, and quartz crystals. There is evidence, too, that uranium may be an important resource for the future, chiefly for nuclear energy.

Brazil has long been known for its diamonds, particularly the black diamond that is found in few other places in the world. Its extreme hardness is more important than its beauty, and it is used mainly for industrial purposes. Other kinds of diamonds for industrial use are prevalent. Only about one third of Brazil's diamonds are fine enough for jewelry. Semiprecious stones abound. In fact, Brazil has produced almost 90 percent of the world's supply of gems such as aquamarines, topazes, amethysts, and tourmalines, and recently has become an important producer of emeralds.

Emerald mine

Brazil would not stand where it does in the production of minerals and gems were it not for the *garimpeiro*, the independent prospector who may spend his entire life roaming the hills, searching for gold, diamonds, and precious stones. It was a wandering *garimpeiro* who discovered Brazil's manganese deposits in Amapá while prospecting for gold during World War II.

Today the government-sponsored Mineral Resources Research Company prepares detailed geological maps and evaluates new deposits of ore and minerals. The company also coordinates operations involving both the government and private industry and sometimes serves as a financing agency.

MAJOR INDUSTRIES IN ACTION

Brazil produces more iron and steel than any other country in Latin America. It supplies a substantial amount of its domestic rolled steel needs. Much of this production goes into the manufacturing of automobiles and into shipbuilding, two industries that were almost unknown in Brazil prior to World War II. The automotive industry was established in order to reduce Brazil's dependence upon foreign imports. The first Brazilian trucks came off the assembly lines in 1957 and the first cars, a year later. Among the non-Brazilian investors in automobile manufacture are General Motors, Chrysler, Ford, Volkswagen, Mercedes-Benz, Toyota, Fiat, and Alfa-Romeo.

The first shipyard in Brazil was built in Rio de Janeiro in the mid-1800s. During the next century, it completed an average of less than one ship a year. Shipbuilding was still a minor industry, employing only about a thousand workers, in the early 1960s. Today the half-dozen shipyards build craft ranging from small fishing vessels and riverboats to oil tankers and refrigerated bulk carriers.

Textiles are vital to Brazil's economy, as they have been since colonial times. But the growth of the industry has depended upon the rise and fall of many other sectors of the economy. The industry started as a group handicraft production system in the eighteenth century. It was semi-industrial, but nothing like the textile industry in England and on the European continent.

During the 1840s, when Brazil was feeling the growing pains of independence, the need arose for cheaper textiles to replace costly imports. Consequently, the first textile mills sprang up in the state of Bahia, followed by others in the states of Rio de Janeiro and São Paulo in the 1870s. The products were of the simplest kind. They were gradually improved and made more sophisticated by the end of the century, largely because of the arrival of European immigrants who were experienced in the manufacture of textiles and clothing.

After World War I, plants were built with greater capacities, some specializing in one or more of the many available vegetable and animal fibers. The production of synthetic fabrics combined

Volkswagen assembly line at São Paulo (left); millworker (right) inspects fabric for defects.

the chemical and fiber industries in Brazil and led to many new developments in manufacturing. The available raw materials include natural fibers, such as cotton, wool, jute, sisal, and silk; chemical fibers, such as viscose and acetate; and synthetics, such as nylon, polyester, and acrylics. Today Brazil's textile industry employs about half a million people, not counting those in the chemical and clothing industries or the farmers and ranchers who produce natural fibers.

THE ENERGY INDUSTRY

Brazil's involvement in the production of energy goes back to the days when her rushing rivers and waterfalls were harnessed to operate crude machines used in the fields and mines. Hydroelectric power offers enormous potential in a land where there is a greater flow of water than anywhere else on earth. Hydroelectric power stations now produce nearly all of Brazil's electricity. Large plants now operate on various rivers including Sao Francisco, and Tocantins, as well as the Itaipu project on the

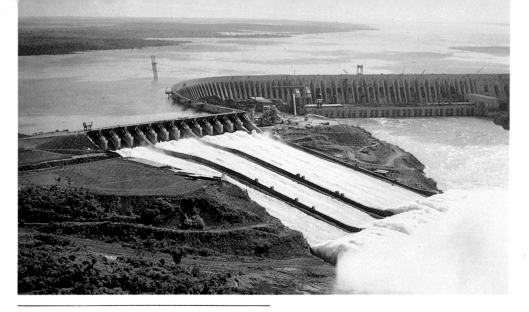

Dams, such as this one at Itaipu, are converting Brazil's water power into usable energy sources.

Paraná River, with the largest such power generators in the world and capable of producing six times as much energy as Egypt's Aswan High Dam on the Nile River.

Brazil has been very slow in exploiting gas and oil and other forms of petroleum. Petrobrás, the national oil company, was not formed until the early 1950s, at a time when crude oil production was only two thousand barrels a day (compared with eight million a day in the United States). In 1976, to help develop oil reserves that could be vast, Brazil, for the first time, invited foreign nations to begin exploration within its borders. Today, Brazil produces about 50 percent of the oil it needs each year. Most of the rest is purchased from the Middle East. Coal and charcoal also provide some energy in Brazil.

TRANSPORTATION

Brazil's size and its jungles and other wilderness areas have for centuries hindered the development of effective transportation systems. Some communities in the interior still can be reached only by riverboats or along the poorest narrow roads. Geography

84

In underdeveloped regions, unpaved roads are common. Even in the
"dry season" muddy conditions can cause trucks to become stuck.

and geology have played their part in making travel slow and
laborious in many places. Yet much of the problem can be traced
directly to a lack of organization and the haphazard methods of
trying to cope with size, distances, and topography.

HIGHWAYS AND RAILROADS

Not until the middle of the twentieth century was a systematic
effort made to create a planned network of surface transportation
in which road, rail, and water facilities were integrated. One of
the drawbacks to creating such a system is the extremely lopsided
spread of the population. Three fourths of the people live within a
radius of about 150 miles (241 kilometers) of the Atlantic coast,
mainly in the southeast in the states of São Paulo, Rio de Janeiro,
Minas Gerais, and Rio Grande do Sul. About two thirds of the
country's land still has a population density of only eighteen
people per square mile. Reaching these isolated groups by modern
and efficient highway systems is not only costly, but in some cases
frustrating, as well as challenging.

Highway from São Paulo to Santos

The first roads were built by Portuguese settlers to link their profitable resources with the larger towns and the ports from which goods were shipped to Europe. Thus, networks of highways emerged in places such as the northeast when the sugar plantations were most active; in the Minas Gerais territory after gold and iron ore were discovered; and in the coffee-growing regions when that crop was beginning to strengthen the economy. Roads were also built for military purposes, to help defend the country against invasion by hostile neighbors or the Spaniards.

The expansion of the highway system is one of the major goals of modern Brazil. Some success has already been achieved, mainly in the construction of major, long-distance arteries. These include the Belém-Brasília highway, built when the new capital was being completed; the Marshal Rondon highway, which connects the state of Acre and the territory of Rondônia in the west to the capital of Mato Grosso; and the east-west Trans-Amazonian highway, connecting Atlantic coast ports with the interior. Brazil's highways are characterized by their length. For example, the Belém-Brasília road is more than 1,300 miles (2,091 kilometers) long. The BR-135 highway, stretching from north to south, is more than 2,300 miles (3,701 kilometers) long.

The construction of railways began in the nineteenth century. Most of the lines were designed to move goods, not passengers. Built largely by British companies, the railways were independent of other transportation facilities and were often isolated, rather than links in a planned network. After World War II, the Brazilian government acquired most of the foreign-owned lines with the idea of building spurs to tie them together in a comprehensive system. Some of these have been constructed and others planned. A federal railway subsidiary, the Brazilian Urban Train Company (CBTU), runs passenger services in the principal cities.

INLAND WATERWAYS

For generations, rivers and streams provided the only means of reaching the Brazilian interior. Building roads was impossible. Even foot trails quickly became overgrown and useless, enveloped in the fast-spreading jungle foliage, mired in mud, or washed out by torrential downpours and floods. Brazil has as many as 30,000 miles (48,270 kilometers) of navigable inland waterways. Some, like the Amazon, are broad enough and deep enough to accommodate oceangoing ships. Others are navigable only by small boat. In some regions heavy rains, floods, and droughts present constantly changing conditions that hamper maritime traffic.

This vast inland waterway system plays an important role in the Brazilian economy, especially in the Amazon Valley and the Paraná Basin. Rivers are often the most effective means of

This landowner flies out to his farm near Sorocaba for an inspection tour.

transporting raw materials from the interior to the ports along the Atlantic coast. Plans to connect some of the key rivers by canals have been underway for many years, but almost nothing has yet been undertaken.

AIR TRANSPORTATION

History books tend to overlook the fact that one of the most successful aeronauts of the early days of flying was a Brazilian. He was Alberto Santos-Dumont who, in 1898, was the first to construct and fly a gasoline-motored airship. Journeying to France, he made aviation history with several lighter-than-air ships that won prizes in international competition. In 1905, he turned to the construction of airplanes and four years later built and piloted a monoplane that was remarkably advanced for its era.

For a short time before World War I, Brazil had a small aviation industry, stimulated by Santos-Dumont and other pioneers. But such endeavors were isolated until after World War II. The lack of a domestic aircraft industry was sorely felt in a country whose land stretched for nearly 3.3 million square miles (8,547,000 square kilometers) and whose rail and highway services to its interior were toally inadequate.

Commercial air routes were first introduced in Brazil in 1927 and were immediately successful, though on a limited basis. Brazil had no training facilities for people who wanted to get into commercial aviation until the early 1940s. Even then, and until the formation of the Technological Institute of Aeronautics, training was conducted partly in the United States.

Private airlines were slow in developing until government support in the 1950s and 1960s led to the formation of new airlines and the expansion of existing lines. By the middle of the 1970s there were four airlines, of which VARIG was by far the largest. Yet the total air fleet at that time was only a little more than one hundred planes. By the 1980s, Brazil's air fleet had grown by 50 percent, not counting small companies that operate domestic air taxi and helicopter services. Brazil has over 125 airports that are used regularly for commercial flights. Brazil's own commercial fleet consists of over 248 aircraft. Most of the international traffic is routed through two airports at Rio de Janeiro, two at São Paulo, one at Brasília, and one at Manaus.

Recently the government established a company called EMBRAER. This company specializes in the design and construction of small aircraft suitable for carrying only twelve to eighteen passengers. The planes can be used for regular service on routes that would not justify larger aircraft. The planes can land at the smaller airports in the interior or mountain regions, or even on the open plains. Another vital step in air transportation has been the installation of one of the most modern flight traffic-control systems in the world, one that will eventually be able to handle the safe movement of more than two thousand planes a day.

Young villagers gather to watch a cockfight.

Chapter 6

CULTURAL ROOTS
AND REWARDS

In the 1960s a director of the Institute of Latin American Studies referred to the "Great Tradition" to explain the uniqueness of Brazilian culture. The origins of its population go back to the Indians, West African slaves, the Portuguese, Spaniards, Germans, British, Italians, and other nationalities. In spite of the country's vastness and mixed heritage, there is a cultural unity that exists in no other major nation on earth. This unity stems directly from the culture inherited from Old-World Europe.

The Brazilian middle and upper classes are the stronghold of the country's cultural life. They have not been changed by class conflicts, economic reversals, or political upheavals, as have groups in most Latin American countries. They have remained constant for generations, maintaining a cultural identity that has characterized Brazil and her people for more than four centuries.

The Great Tradition is very solid. Its foundations lie not only in history but also in the old written codes of philosophy, theology, science, art, literature, music, and law. Yet it is also remarkably flexible, able to absorb those cultures that come to it from the outside. Consider for example, the Amazon natives, who were there long before the arrival of the Portuguese explorers, and the

West African slaves, who were imported against their will. Aspects of the art and music of both these cultures have become integral elements of the total Brazilian culture.

This cultural unity binds together all classes, with relatively few exceptions. Although those people who are illiterate or who live in isolation or poverty may be incapable of expressing their cultural heritage, they are deeply affected by it and reflect it in their outlooks and judgments.

RELIGIOUS BONDS AND BELIEFS

One of the strong features of Brazil's cultural solidarity is religion. Of those who profess a faith, more than 90 percent claim Roman Catholicism. This faith, like the general culture, mingles many elements. It is not uncommon to find Catholicism that seems to have been influenced by Indians, by the descendants of the West Africans, by spiritualism or by other faiths. Brazil's religious culture is so unique that it has generated a popular saying—"God is a Brazilian."

The Brazilian idea of religious faith tends to be tolerant and accepting. The explorers who first encountered tribes of Indians in the interior often became intrigued by their simple brand of faith. The Indians viewed the jungles as a haven for all kinds of spirits, sometimes in the form of animals, oftentimes unseen in the dark recesses of the foliage. Many of these spirits were evil, but others brought good luck. A few were mischievous, even playful and humorous. Instead of trying to prove to the Indians that such creatures did not exist, the settlers tended to accept this religious culture as something that existed, just as surely as did the rivers and forests. Seldom did they try to force their own Christian

Yanomami Indian (left) picks papaya in the Amazon rain forest. These Indians have lived in the jungles for centuries.

doctrines upon the Indians. As a result, Brazilian life and culture, and even some aspects of religion, incorporate some of these native traditions. There has never been any outright suppression of faiths and beliefs, which is why so many have mingled comfortably and lastingly in Brazil.

THE STATE AS A UNIFYING FORCE

Brazilians of all racial, national, and economic backgrounds share the deep-seated belief that they are a single *people*. Together, they share a common history, common goals and ideals, common tastes, and a common outlook on life and the future. Sociologists have identified Brazilians as sharing certain traits of behavior, social values, and even a kind of national sense of humor. These traits seem to develop naturally within the Brazilian environment.

Brazilians have created their own art, music, literature, theater, and architecture, often with the support of the government. Thus, this sense of unity has become strongly ingrained. It carries over into a way of life that includes a great interest in soccer, tennis, basketball, and other sports; the spontaneous creation and enjoyment of musical groups and small popular orchestras; and special talents in architecture and all fields of creativity that delight the eye, as well as the ear.

THE VISUAL ARTS

Anthropologists have discovered numerous forms of art created by the native Indians long before the discovery of Brazil by Pedro Álvares Cabral in 1500. European art was almost nonexistent until the arrival of the Dutch in the 1630s. Several artists among these settlers painted the first Brazilian scenes, partly to show people back home in The Netherlands what this new land and its people looked like. Paintings, however, were rare. The best surviving examples of artistic creativity in the late seventeenth century and for almost the next one hundred years are the architecture, sculpture, and religious pictures of the period. They were created mainly in the old mining towns like Ouro Preto and Diamantina and in Salvador in Bahia when it was the first capital.

The most noted Brazilian artist of the colonial period was Antônio Francisco Lisboa (1730-1814), better known as Aleijadinho (the Little Cripple). He was a mulatto, the son of a black slave from West Africa. Aleijadinho was so crippled by disease that he could not grip the tools he used for his sculptures and had to have chisels and mallets strapped to his hands. He was extremely prolific, turning out hundreds of remarkable works of art—statues, carved pulpits, church portals, and other stone and wood sculptures still admired today.

The first known Brazilian portrait painter was Manuel da

Aleijadinho's wood carving of the Last Supper (left) and Portinari's religious painting (right) reflect the nation's artistic heritage

Cunha, a former slave. During the late eighteenth and early nineteenth centuries, he was a kind of artistic pioneer who demonstrated that native artistic talents should be encouraged. In 1809, King John VI recognized this potential and invited the French to send an art mission to Brazil to foster the development of art. Brazilian art began to flourish. Rio de Janeiro soon became the artistic center of the country. Two of the leading painters of the middle and latter parts of the nineteenth century were Pedro Américo and Victor Meireles. They painted huge canvases depicting historic events and scenes, particularly during the Empire period.

Art remained somewhat primitive in Brazil. This lack of sophistication helped the Brazilians develop their own styles and art forms without copying Europeans. Then, in the 1920s, native Brazilians began to develop a new school of modern art, pioneered by a local artist named Anita Malfati and several European artists who had migrated to Brazil.

The result was that many young Brazilian artists were suddenly inspired. One of the most provocative painters to emerge was Cândido Portinari (1903-1962). Portinari painted the well-known murals on war and peace in the United Nations General Assembly Building in New York City.

Brazilian sculpture followed much the same pattern. Initially, during the colonial period, it was an interesting blend of the baroque influence from Old-World Portugal and figures and symbols from the Indians and the West African slaves. The best examples of early church carvings are found in some of the religious buildings built in the state of Bahia during the eighteenth century. Other fine examples can be seen in the ornate woodwork of the São Bento monastery in Rio de Janeiro. The nineteenth century saw an increasing development of native sculpture, often motivated by architectural planning. When Belo Horizonte was planned and built in the 1890s, for example, it stimulated artistic contributions not only from architects, but also from painters and sculptors.

A similar achievement took place when Brasília was built. Many of the country's most noted artists and designers worked on this immense project. Included among them were the city planner, Lúcio Costa; the architect, Oscar Niemeyer; and dozens of painters and sculptors who created murals, statues, and other works.

LITERARY ACHIEVEMENTS

Unlike the visual arts, which progressed erratically and often regionally, Brazilian literature can be traced through four distinct periods. Each is related in part to four different stages in the country's political and social history. These four literary periods are the colonial period, from the country's early years until its independence in 1822; the romantic period, paralleling the fifty-seven years of the empire, until the 1880s; the post-romantic period, covering the first few decades of the new republic; and the modern period, which began in the early 1920s.

Poetry was the first literary form to make a deep and lasting impression on the Brazil of the colonial period. Two poets of eminence at that time were Gregório de Matos Guerra and Basílio de Gama. Gregório de Matos wrote sharply satirical poems in the latter half of the seventeenth century. Basílio da Gama's poems were epics, telling dramatic stories in a manner similar to some of the epic poems of European literature. He wrote during the second half of the eighteenth century, at a time when a group of poets in the Minas Gerais School were inspiring Brazilian dreams of independence.

During the romantic period, poets continued to dominate literature, many using Indians and slaves in their themes. These poets, many of whom died while they were still young, were poor. They could relate to lives of hardship and the enduring struggle for freedom. A typical member of this school was Antônio de Castro Alves, the "Poet of Slavery," who demanded that all slaves be set free. Castro Alves died in 1871 at the age of twenty-four.

The novelists of the romantic era took their themes from folklore on one hand and the urban way of life on the other. José de Alencar (1821-1877) wrote popular novels on these subjects, treating them in a very romantic fashion. An uncharacteristic author of this period was Manuel Antônio de Almeida, who died at the age of thirty in 1861. His use of realism in his one novel made him a pioneer. But he was ahead of his time. Almeida's novel received little attention until the twentieth century.

The romantic school was followed by a period when writers began to turn to realism. Once again, poetry was the dominant form. The poems were characterized by rigid form and flawless workmanship. Realistic novels were written, too. Aluísio de

Azevedo was the first Brazilian novelist to write about social changes in the lives of the people. Near the end of the 1800s, the critical essay explored the works of other writers and the whole field of the arts.

BIRTH AND GROWTH OF THE MODERN SCHOOL

In a sense, the modern period really came about with a single event, known as Modern Art Week. Celebrated in 1922, its impact spread swiftly throughout the country, influencing art and literature alike. It would be erroneous to say that the single "week" suddenly caused a revolutionary change in the arts. Rather, it was a kind of symbol for a movement that slowly had been gathering steam. It became significant when authors began to use words and language in an impressionistic style to communicate and express their messages.

The modern Brazilian novel, which developed after the 1920s, focused strongly on social problems. The most widely read authors wrote about the challenges and hardships of life in the regions of the country they knew best. Jorge Amado's novels depict the social problems of blacks on the cocoa plantations of Bahia, or fishermen in the small northeastern villages, or middle-class workers in Salvador. He was an early exponent of an Afro-Brazilian school of literature that used dialogues between humans and gods, not unlike the techniques used by ancient Greek poets.

Jorge Mateus de Lima was a poet of the Afro-Brazilian school. This mystic poet influenced many other writers from the 1930s until he died in 1953. Social historians also began to find a solid place in the literature of the modern era. Gilberto Freyre

Brazilian musicians play Indian instruments at an outdoor market in Liberdade, the Japanese district of São Paulo.

pioneered this school of sociology, writing with a strong style and clarity. Sociological subjects, which had formerly been considered of interest only to professionals and scholars, were now being read by the general public.

MUSIC AND THE THEATER

Brazil has always had music. Natives had evolved primitive instruments and mystical chants to influence the spirits who dwelled in the jungles around them. Settlers from Portugal introduced European music. The music was sung and played primarily in worship, first in the small churches of the northeast and later in those of Minas Gerais and Rio de Janeiro.

No one knows exactly when it happened, but the music from Portugal and other European countries began to blend with

Indian music and later with the songs brought by slaves from West Africa. This blending of musical cultures has continued to the present day.

Early records indicate that organized music schools existed as early as the late sixteenth century in several towns in Bahia in the northeast. Apparently they were at least partially religious in nature, training people to play and sing church music. Folk music was commonplace and was heard whenever people got together for festivals and dancing.

A more formalized interest in music began after the arrival of the royal family from Portugal in 1807. Marcos Portugal, a noted composer who was a member of the royal court, established educational programs in music. Equally influential was a priest named José Maurício. One of the best-known Brazilian composers of his day, he wrote more than four hundred musical compositions, including a famous Requiem Mass in B-flat.

For a time, the Italian influence pervaded the music of Brazil, creating great interest in the opera. One of the major musicians in Brazil in the nineteenth century was Antônio Carlos Gomes, who composed a number of notable operas in the Italian style. About this time, there was a split in the ranks of the musical pioneers of the day. One school, represented by musicians like Gomes, preferred the traditional European music. Others, like Francisco Manuel, felt that music needed a new vitality—Brazilian in nature and treatment.

After the nineteenth century, music tended more to the Brazilian, adopting themes from the native folklore and dance. As was true with literature and art, the year 1922 (with its Modern Art Week) was a pivotal point in Brazilian music. The modern era was to begin. One of the musicians most affected was thirty-five-

Samba dancers parade during Rio de Janeiro's carnival.

year-old Heitor Villa-Lobos. A prolific composer, Villa-Lobos blended the music of rural and wilderness Brazil into modern symphonic compositions. By the time he died in 1959, he had produced about seventeen hundred works. Many of them achieved worldwide acclaim.

Brazilian popular music is a rich blend of past and present. The dance music of the samba and its more recent offshoot, the bossa nova, has an almost magical appeal to people of all ages and all nationalities. It originated in the batuque, an African form of the dance. In colonial days slaves dancing the batuque kept the beat with their African drums. Today throughout Brazil, every city, every town, every village has its samba schools.

The theater in Brazil has not yet had the impact that the visual arts, music, and literature have had on the culture of the country.

Schoolchildren in small school. Primary education is the responsibility of state and local governments and in many areas there are not enough funds or teachers to meet the educational needs of the people.

Although acting and drama go back to the early colonial days, many of the performances were religious or ritualistic in nature—visual and physical expressions of faith. At the end of the eighteenth century, the theater became popular among the wealthy inhabitants of mining towns in Minas Gerais. At Manaus, during the rubber boom, opera flourished for a time. But these were short-lived, isolated instances. After Brazil achieved independence, more sophisticated theatrical companies were organized in the large cities, such as Rio and São Paulo, and are quite active today.

EDUCATION

Under the Brazilian constitution, education is "the right of everyone and the duty of the state." About 80 percent of Brazil's adults can read and write. However, educational levels vary widely throughout the country. Generally they are higher in southern Brazil and lower in the northeast. Children from ages seven through fourteen must attend school, but many leave after completing the requirement and begin to work. Most of these children are from poor rural families.

Educational opportunities for the young are better in Brazil's larger cities.

Many rural areas also lack sufficient schools and teachers. In some of these areas the government broadcasts instruction programs over the radio. University students also do volunteer teaching and there are widespread government programs to teach adults how to read and write.

In Brazil, primary education is the responsibility of state and municipal authorities. Secondary schools are largely owned and operated by private individuals and institutions, including the Roman Catholic church and other denominations. There are a number of fine universities in Brazil, but they are limited in size and enrollment. Many young people attend universities in North America and Europe, especially if they are going into the professions or seeking careers in fields of advanced technology.

The educational system in Brazil continues to improve, but it will do so only at an immense cost and with the dedicated efforts of educators who can accept the challenge.

The people of Brazil reflect their mixed ethnic and racial heritage.

Chapter 7

THE MANY FACES
OF BRAZIL

It is as difficult to depict a "typical" Brazilian in words or pictures as it is to portray an average European. However, certain factors can be used as guidelines. The first is that average Brazilians are *young*. At least 35 percent of the population is under the age of fifteen while nearly 58 percent range between fifteen and fifty-nine. Another characteristic is that they would probably represent a blend of several heritages—European, West African, and native Indian.

The people of Brazil are a complex mixture of many ethnic, racial, and economic backgrounds. The blending is far from uniform, yet it continues to approach uniformity because Brazilians are constantly migrating from one region of their country to another. This intermixture reduces regional differences from one generation to the next.

Although there is a solid base of unity in the matter of national types and traits, the similarities and differences can best be seen by examining each of the important backgrounds of the modern-day Brazilian people.

THE WILDERNESS INDIANS

The aboriginal population of what is now Brazil was very small and thinly spread. Before the landings of the first Portuguese explorers, this region, covering half of the continent of South America, probably held no more than 1.5 million Indians, scattered in small tribes in regions such as Amazonia, the jungles of Mato Grosso, the interior highlands, the prairies of the south, and the land along the Atlantic coast.

There were hundreds of tribes, almost like individual families, many of which have long since lost their identities or any traces of their early cultures. In the Amazon River basin alone, there were at least fifty distinct tribes, with names ranging alphabetically from the Aikas and Amahuacas to the Cayapos, Kyabis, Omaguas, Quechuas, Ticunas, Xavantes, and the Yurimaguas.

Like all native Americans, they were descended from the Paleo-Mongoloids. These were primitive peoples who lived in the Far East in the region later known as Mongolia. During the last Ice Age, somewhere between thirty thousand and seventy thousand years ago, they migrated into what is now Siberia and crossed over the frozen Bering Strait to Alaska. Over many thousands of years, these peoples, collectively known as Indians, spread across North America, along the isthmus of Central America, and into all of South America. Archaeologists and anthropologists have documented this immense historical migration. The tribes of the Amazon and the other wilderness areas of Brazil clearly have features and traits that are Mongoloid. These include high cheekbones, black eyes, the Oriental fold of the eyelid, and lack of beards. There are also Mongoloid elements in their culture. Many of the parallels are striking, such as the use of the blowgun, the

Yanomami Indian makes a palm leaf basket (left) in the Amazon forest. In the face of the young male (right) one can see Mongoloid traits—high cheekbones, black eyes, an Oriental fold of the eyelid, and the lack of beard.

playing of musical panpipes, and the habit of chewing lime or ashes.

It has been estimated that these primitive peoples finally reached South America at least twenty thousand years ago. They were, therefore, well established in Brazil at the time of its discovery not quite five hundred years ago. Being spread far and wide, the Indians of South America never grouped into the tribal masses found in parts of Mexico and the United States.

Within the boundaries of what is now Brazil, there were said to be four different linguistic groups—that is, four basic tribes identifiable by their spoken language and symbols. They were the Tupí-Guarani, Je, Karib, and Aruak. Of these, the Tupí became the best known, since they lived in the northeastern coastal region where the original Portuguese settlements were founded. The Tupí, in fact, became associated in the minds of the settlers as being representative of all native Indians in Brazil. From the very beginning, there was an intermixture of Portuguese and Indian blood. As there were far more males than females among the earliest settlers, many of the men took Indian women as wives.

The Guarani, related to the Tupí, inhabited the lands along the River Plate in the south and southwest. They became well known to the Brazilians who settled in this part of the country and a similar intermixture took place. In fact, Tupí names and backgrounds were encountered in many parts of Brazil—in contrast to most of the other groups of Indians, who were scattered and little known.

Unfortunately, although the native Indians have contributed to the stock of the Brazilian people, many of the Indians were persecuted by the settlers. History is filled with accounts of massacres of Indians, as well as of wholesale exploitation and slavery. Natives were understandably hostile when white explorers suddenly appeared in their territory. That hostility, intensified by terror at the sight of guns, swords, and other weapons, often incited them to quick attack. And, almost invariably, whenever bands of intruders were killed, their survivors retaliated by killing the natives, often by the thousands. Not content with simply killing, both sides frequently resorted to torture and atrocities.

Only recently has this grim warfare abated. At the beginning of the twentieth century, an Indian Protection Service began to focus attention on the plight of the natives. It was the brainchild of Colonel Cândido Mariano da Silva Rondon, himself part Indian and a noted Amazon explorer. He set out to accomplish four goals: respect for Indians and tribal institutions; guarantee of permanent ownership by Indians of the land they live on and exclusive rights to the natural resources that exist on those lands; preservation of the Indians' cultural and biological balance in their contacts with other Brazilian groups and societies; and protection of the Indians against sudden changes in their environment by outside forces.

Although there have been occasional charges of mismanagement and corruption since the formation of the Indian Protection Service, the Indians have taken a more rightful place in Brazilian society. Significantly, and ironically, Indian customs and cultures have long been accepted and assimilated into the lives of Brazilians, no matter how fiercely the natives and the whites were slaughtering each other along the frontiers. Once Indians were brought into Brazilian society, either through capture or intermarriage, they exerted their influence on it.

The blending of the Indian strains and customs with the European was often enhanced by writers of the day, who described the "noble savages" and, in some cases, asserted that they possessed qualities that put their white conquerors to shame. This attitude became widely accepted and was one of the positive forces in the blending of these dissimilar heritages.

Today's Brazilians may be just as proud of their Indian heritage as they are of their European origins. Some of the most honored family names in the country include words and names borrowed from Indians, particularly from the Tupí language, the one most familiar to Europeans who migrated to Brazil.

INFLUENCES FROM WEST AFRICA

In colonial days, very few blacks arrived in Brazil by choice. They were brought in as slaves, first to work on sugar plantations. After the middle of the sixteenth century, the need for laborers was critical. Portuguese immigrants came to Brazil to make their

In Salvador this young boy (left) and the women at the old port market (right) reflect their African heritage.

fortunes or escape some form of tyranny. But they had no desire for hard labor. The Indians who had been brought to the plantations, either for hire or as slaves, had no talent for working the land. And they rebelled at being regimented. So the only recourse was to import slaves. Most of these unwilling immigrants came from the area of West Africa between the Senegal and Niger rivers—the same slave source used by American plantation owners in the South and in the West Indies.

It was not long before West Africans began to outnumber the Indians in Brazil. By 1825, the total population of Brazil was computed at four million. Of this number, almost half were listed as Negroes. The whites numbered less than one million, and the rest were either of mixed blood or Indians. By the time the importation of slaves was outlawed in 1850, and certainly by the time slavery was abolished in 1888, blacks were already beginning to mix with whites, with Indians, and with the existing mixed strains.

The Brazilian reputation for racial tolerance resulted in a far greater and faster assimilation and crossbreeding than in any other country in history. As was the case with the Indians, intermarriage retained, rather than rejected, many of the religious beliefs and cultures of the former slaves. Families with African heritages were positive blends of the racial strains that had been inherited. Unlike other countries, too, Brazil has never had any laws against racial intermarriages. Because the national philosophy rejects the idea of racist concepts, people who are dark-skinned face little discrimination—at least not by their Brazilian peers. If there is any stigma at all attached to blacks, it is an economic one, relating directly to slave days and the obvious association of color with abject poverty. Yet even that disadvantage has steadily diminished and has almost vanished.

The only region where there are still large proportions of blacks is in the state of Bahia, where their West African ancestors first arrived. Some communities may have two or three blacks or mulattoes for every white. Yet even these proportions are changing as the mixture continues and the "typical" Brazilian emerges. The people of Rio have long had a heavy African strain. In São Paulo and Paraná, where there were relatively few slaves from Africa, at least one person in eight is estimated to have a trace of Negro blood. Even in the state of Santa Catarina in the south, where the proportion is the lowest in the country, almost one person in every fifteen can trace partial ancestry back to a West African.

Difficult though it was for a West African to adapt from slavery to freedom and a job with pay, many former slaves made the transition with remarkable success. Some achieved greatness in various fields and became highly respected in their communities. As was pointed out by William L. Schurz, a specialist on Latin America, a quarter of a century ago, the former slave "would not have to contend with any segregation policies. . . would not be told where he would have to live or with whom he might associate or marry. Enough of his kind had already demonstrated their capacity for high accomplishment that he need suffer from no inferiority complex by reason of his color or his servile background. . . .

"He was starting at the bottom of the economic ladder, but at least no one on the higher rungs would trample on his fingers, and they might even reach down and give him a helpful lift. There was an immense fund of good will for him to draw on, and if he were willing to make the effort, the future could hold the same rewards as for any other Brazilian."

THE PORTUGUESE

The Portuguese, of course, were the ones who started the whole chain reaction through the discovery of Brazil and the voyages of exploration and settlement that followed. It is only natural, then, that the Portuguese heritage should be the dominant factor in shaping the nature of the Brazilian people. From the Portugal of the sixteenth and seventeenth centuries came the characteristics that survive today. These include a tolerant attitude toward races and religions, a sense of humor, patience, an aversion to violence, and a certain leaning toward both the melancholy and the

This family dinner includes rice, salad, and citrus fruit.

romantic. Typical Brazilians reveal all of these traits to greater or lesser degrees. Underneath these characteristics lie a certain boldness and daring and a persistence that gets things done through an inherent sense of teamwork. In the past, these qualities were what made Portugal, despite its tiny size, the greatest maritime nation in the world for more than a century. In the present, they are what made it possible to build an entire modern city, Brasília, in less than a decade. They are qualities that inspired the geniuses who have created some of the country's finest art, architecture, music, and literature.

The fact that the Portuguese were at home on endless stretches of ocean may also have played a part in shaping a unique facet of the Brazilian nature. From the very beginning, Brazilians have accepted and lived comfortably with the vastness of their land, as though it were an ocean on which they could navigate at will. They are neither daunted nor awed by rivers and jungles that are among the greatest in the world, broad plains that stretch from horizon to horizon, or other geographical superlatives. A great deal of internal migration takes place, from one state or territory to another. Yet the Brazilian seems always at home.

Surfers at the beach at Ipanema, Rio de Janiero

THE DIFFERENCES

An accurate picture of "typical" Brazilians with certain common characteristics and traits must also show that there are differences. Some are regional in nature; others relate to social standing or to economic positions. A good example is that of the *carioca* who lives in Rio de Janeiro versus the *paulista* who lives in São Paulo. In the eyes of the *carioca*, the citizens of São Paulo are materialists or workaholics, setting their sights far too much on money and career. In the eyes of the *paulista,* the inhabitants of Rio are lazy or incompetent, living from one day to another with no plans for the future.

Both these types are in contrast to the *Nordestinos* of the northeast region, particularly in the state of Bahia. *Nordestinos* are noted for being romantic, sentimental, talkative, and gifted with lively imaginations. They are quite unlike the *Sertanejos,* who live to the west and away from the coast, and who are just the opposite—unromantic, unimaginative, and untalkative. Other types are easily recognizable. Brazilians from the interior highlands, like native New Englanders, are cautious and laconic, and like to rib each other with a straight-faced brand of humor.

Pedestrian shopping mall in São Paulo

The *gaúchos*, the cowboys of the southern plains, are rugged types, as frank and earthy as their counterparts in the United States.

The people of Brazil have largely absorbed the other foreigners who came to their shores from Europe, the Orient, North America, and elsewhere. Still, there are a few pockets where non-Brazilians predominate—Italian, Spaniard, Dutch, German, Chinese, or Japanese. The Italians, for example, arrived in great numbers—more than a million—in the 1880s and 1890s, largely attracted to the coffee *fazendas* in the state of São Paulo. Later they arrived in the state of Rio Grande do Sul, where they started vineyards. About half a million Spaniards migrated to Brazil prior to World War I, settling in the region near the River Plate.

However, if history prevails, even the most recently arrived immigrants will eventually be absorbed into the national culture and become almost unrecognizable as anything but Brazilians.

That is the way it is in this giant land. Huge and sprawling and varied though it may be, Brazil exerts its unifying influence over all newcomers, until they are no longer strangers but, first and foremost, Brazilians. That is how it was in the beginning—and how it still is today.

MAP KEY

(*Does not appear on map; key shows general location)

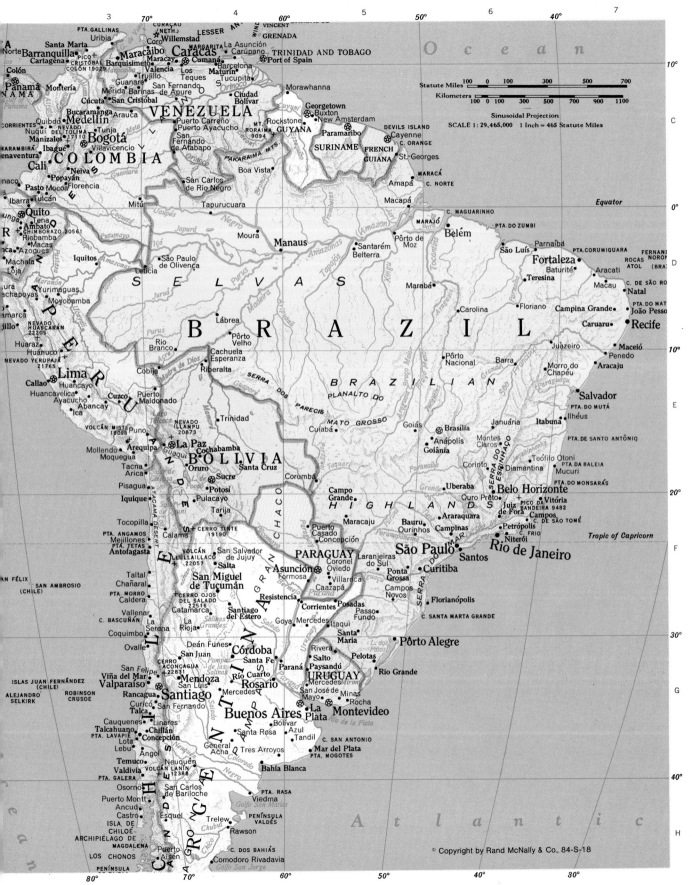

MINI-FACTS AT A GLANCE

GENERAL INFORMATION

Official Name: Federative Republic of Brazil *(República Federativa do Brazil)*

Capital: Brasília

Official Language: Portuguese

Government: Brazil's government is a federal republic with twenty-six states, and one federal district.

In the Brazilian government there are three branches—the executive, legislative, and judicial. The president, whose term is for five years, is elected directly by the people—as also is a vice-president. The president appoints federal officials and judges with the consent of the Senate. The constitution adopted in 1988 calls for direct elections, more political parties, the abolition of censorship and broader economic powers for Congress than the 1967 constitution.

Congress is made up of 81 members of the Senate and 503 members of the Chamber of Deputies. Senators serve eight-year terms and deputies are elected to four-year terms. Three senators are elected from each state. The number of deputies a state has depends on its population, but each state has at least three. Senators and deputies can be elected to more than one consecutive term. A president cannot serve consecutive terms.

Each state has its own constitution, governor, and legislature. The governors and state legislatures are elected directly by the people. All literate citizens between the ages of eighteen and seventy must vote. People over seventy and those who are illiterate have the option of not voting.

Flag: The national flag has a yellow diamond centered on a green background. On the diamond is a blue sphere with twenty-three white stars. The sphere is crossed with a band bearing the motto *"Ordem e Progresso"* ("Order and Progress").

National Song: *"Hino Nacional"*

Religion: Brazil is 90 percent Roman Catholic, according to the 1990 census.

Money: The basic unit of money is the *cruzeiro,* written CR $1,00. (The comma is used as a decimal point.) It is divided into 100 *centavos.*

Weights and Measures: The metric system has been used since 1862. Ancient measurements are still sometimes used in rural areas.

Population: 163,949,000 (1994 estimate), with 76.9 percent urban, 23.1 rural.

Cities:

São Paulo	9,480,427	Brasília	1,596,274
Rio de Janeiro	5,336,179	Recife	1,290,149
Salvador	2,056,013	Curitiba	1,290,142
Belo Horizonte	2,048,861	Porto Alegre	1,262,631

(Population figures 1991 preliminary census)

GEOGRAPHY

Highest Point: Pico da Neblina, 9,888 ft. (3,014 m)

Lowest Point: Sea level

Coastline: 6,019 mi. (9,687 km)

Rivers: The Amazon River and its tributaries have more water and drain more land than any other river system in the world. The Amazon runs for 1,962 mi. (3,158 km) in Brazil. The second most important river system is the Paraguay-Paraná-Plata. It runs for about 2,050 mi. (3,299 km). The São Francisco River, the third most important river system, runs 1,800 mi. (2,897 km) and is the chief route to the interior.

Mountains: Brazil has few mountains. Almost half of the nation's territory consists of plains and lowlands. However, there are some areas where mountains do exist. For example, the Eastern Highlands altitudes usually range between 2,500 (762 m) and 2,800 ft. (853 m). Within these uplands is also the Serra do Espinhaço, a mountain range that reaches altitudes as high as 3,500 (1,066 m) to 4,200 ft. (1,280 m).

Climate: Most of Brazil lies in the tropics; only the southern "handle" is in the temperate zone. Yet, the climate is comfortable in most regions of the country. Even in the Amazon, the temperature rarely climbs into the 90s F. (32° C), largely because of the heavy rainfall that occurs during the hottest months of the year. The only section of Brazil that could be called torrid is in the northeast, where temperatures of 100° F. (38° C) are frequent during the dry season.

Along the Atlantic coast, from Recife in the north to Rio de Janeiro, temperatures are seldom unbearable. In Rio, for example, the temperature in the warmest months (November through March) seldom gets above 80° F. (27° C), and in the coldest months rarely drops below 65° F. (18° C). To the north, sea breezes moderate the climate. Inland, especially in the central plains, the altitude keeps the temperatures lower than might be expected. And in the regions where there are low mountains, the climate compares favorably with New England summers.

Although rainfall varies greatly, from the heavy rainfall of the Amazon to the northeast where drought is often a problem, most of Brazil has moderate rainfall. Most precipitation occurs in the summers, between December and April. Winters tend to be dry and sunny. In the south, snow falls, although seldom very heavily.

Greatest Distances: North to south—2,684 mi. (4,319 km)
East to west—2,689 mi. (4,328 km)

Area: 3,286,487 sq. mi. (8,511,965 km²)

NATURE

Vegetation: There are seven distinct types of vegetation. In the south are forests and grasslands. In the Pantanal to the southwest there is a floodplain with a mixture of wet savannas and palms. Most of the interior is covered with woodland savannas, known as *campo cerrado*, suitable for crops only when properly plowed and fertilized. To the north is the great rain forest, the *selva*, where foliage is thick and the rainfall constant. Scattered around the country are deciduous forests. The region known as the *várzea*, great plains in the north regularly covered by floodwaters, is among the most fertile lands in South America.

Animals: The Amazon plain has about 700 species of mammals and 1,800 varieties of birds. Its rivers and swamps contain as many as 1,500 species of fish and other aquatic creatures. There are several species of the cat family in Brazil, including the jaguar. There are also sloths, anteaters, tapir, armadillos, wild boar, jungle deer, monkeys, moss-backed turtles, snakes, and rodents. Manatees live in the Amazon along with the pirarucú, sharks, and sawfish; other river dwellers include electric eels, piranhas, and giant horned catfish.

EVERYDAY LIFE

Food: There are many varieties of Brazilian food, depending on the region. Brazilians do not eat vegetables very often, nor do they eat potatoes; they prefer rice instead. Other staples include beans, squash, and cabbage. For appetizers, they eat olives (especially Portuguese black olives), radishes, and carrots.

Some favorite dishes were devised by poor people to make the most of what food they could find. The Bahian dish called *vatapá*, for example, consists of pieces of shrimp and fish, mixed with palm oil and coconut milk and pieces of bread. It is served over rice and was originally eaten by slaves. Another Bahian dish, called *sarapatel*, is made of liver and the heart of a pig or a sheep, and is mixed with the fresh blood of either animal plus tomatoes, peppers, and onions.

In Rio de Janeiro the favorite dish is *feijoada*, a stew made of black beans, chunks of beef, pork, sausages, chops, and sometimes pigs' ears and tails. This is served over rice and with a bright green boiled leaf called *couve* and slices of oranges.

In the northeast, refrigeration is a luxury. Consequently, many people eat dried meat with beans or some green vegetable. Before cooking the meat, which is heavily salted and dried in the sun to preserve it, it first must be soaked overnight.

Still another dish is *galleto al primo canto*, which translates as a young rooster that has crowed for the first time. The rooster is cut into pieces, placed on a spit and basted with white wine and oil. This meal is usually accompanied by red wine.

Brazilian beer is excellent. Brazilians also make good wine. A favorite alcoholic drink is *cachaça* which is made from sugarcane. When mixed with lemon juice or an orangish fruit called *maracujá*, it becomes a *batida*, which is used to create an appetite or aid digestion.

Housing: In the cities, there are many high-rise buildings. Farm families often live in small houses made of woven branches plastered with mud, or houses of stone and mortar covered with stucco and lime. Roofs usually have clay tiles. In the Amazon, people live in huts made of thatched palm leaves and built on stilts.

Holidays: (National)

New Year's Day, January 1	Independence Day, September 7
Good Friday	All Souls' Day, November 2
Tiradentes Day, April 21	Proclamation of the Republic, November 15
Labor Day, May 1	Christmas, December 25

Culture: There is a cultural unity in Brazil that exists in no other major nation. This unity stems directly from the culture inherited from Old-World Europe.

Anthropologists have discovered many art forms created by the native Indians. Brazilian sculpture during the colonial period was a mixture of the European with the symbolism of the Indians and West African slaves. The best examples of early church carvings are found in the state of Bahia. The nineteenth century saw the development of native sculpture. In the 1950s, when Brasília was built, there were modern acomplishments by artists such as the architect Oscar Niemeyer.

In the 1920s, native Brazilians began to develop a new school of modern art. One of the most provocative painters in this period was Candido Portinari, who later did the War and Peace mural at the United Nations in New York.

In literary art forms, Gregório de Matos and Basílio da Gama were important early poets. In the romantic period, poets often used slave or Indian themes. Novelists of the same period, such as José de Alencar, derived themes from folklore and urban life. The romantic period was followed by a switch to realism. One of the best-known authors to write in this style was Aluísio de Azevedo.

The 1920s saw a growing wave of artistic innovation. The Brazilian novel that evolved after the 1920s focused on social problems. Jorge Amado was an important novelist of the time.

The first music of Brazil was folk music and the religious music. By the twentieth century, Brazilian music was more independent. One of the most famous of modern Brazilian composers was Heitor Villa-Lobos. Brazilian popular music has also gained worldwide popularity. The samba and the bossa nova have their origins in African slave dances.

Sports and Recreation: Soccer is a national passion. In fact, national teams have been world soccer champions three times. A sport that is purely Brazilian is the *capoeira*. It has elements of fighting, dancing, and judo all rolled into one. Other popular Brazilian activities include mountain climbing, water-skiing, underwater diving, horse racing, and fishing

Communication: In 1988 Brazil had over three hundred daily newspapers. Most have small circulations. There are no national newspapers, but the papers with the largest circulations are *O Día, Folha de São Paulo,* and *Journal da Tarde.*

There are three kinds of radio and TV stations—government-run, commercial, and religious backed. In 1991 there were 2,700 radio stations and 119 TV stations.

Transportation: Brazil has the largest inland waterway system in the world. There are about seven hundred river ports and thirty-six seaports, five of which are privately owned. The largest seaports are Santos, Rio de Janeiro, and Paranaguá.

There are 18,506 mi. (29,783 km) of railroad track in Brazil, of which 802 mi. (1,607 km) are electric. The government is planning to expand the railway system, including the building of a new line between São Paulo and Belo Horizonte.

Roads link Brasília with every section of the country. In 1990 there were 1,037,738 mi. (1,670,000 km) of roads in Brazil. Highways carry most of the freight and passengers in the country.

Over long distances, air travel is the most practical. There are four major commerical airlines in Brazil—VARIC, Cruzeiro do Sul, Vasp, and Trans-Brasil.

Schools: Education is free and compulsory for children aged eight to fourteen. About 80 percent of adults can read and write. Educational levels vary throughout the country.

The Brazilian system of education includes eight years of primary school, three to four years of second grade or middle school, and secondary school (university level study). Since 1971, the second grade has focused on vocational training. Courses of study are divided into hours rather than years, a system which allows students to learn at their own pace.

Secondary (university) education is free in official schools. The federal government is responsible for higher education, while state and municipal governments are in charge of primary and middle schools. There are many private schools in Brazil, but as of 1980 forty-five of the sixty-five universities were state run.

The school year runs from March to the middle of December.

Health: Many diseases, such as smallpox, malaria, yellow fever, and plague, have been brought under control. In the 1970s, however, there were still many cases of influenza, dysentery, and measles, among other contagious diseases. Other diseases, such as hookworm and schistosomiasis, are prevalent in remote areas. In 1981, a nationwide program called *Pró-saúde* was launched to provide more hospital beds, clinics, and better sanitary conditions.

Principal Products:
Agriculture: Coffee, sugar, rice, cotton, rubber, cocoa, cattle, pigs, wool, jute, sisal, silk, bananas, oranges, tobacco, rubber, maize, cassava, castor beans, and wheat
Manufacturing: Automobiles, shipbuilding, textiles, petrochemicals
Mining: Iron ore, bauxite, manganese, nickel, tin, tungsten, quartz crystals, uranium, diamonds, aquamarines, topazes, amethysts, tourmalines, emeralds, niobium, and thorium, gold, phosphates, crude oil, platinum.

IMPORTANT DATES

1494 — Pope Alexander VI divides the New World between Portugal and Spain

1500 — Pedro Álvares Cabral discovers Brazil for the Portuguese; first settlement at Salvador

1507 — Second Portuguese colony begun at São Vicente

1532 — São Vicente founded; sugarcane introduced there

1549 — Salvador in the state of Bahia becomes capital of Brazil

1580 — Philip II of Spain claims the throne of Portugal and unites the two countries

1630 — The Dutch invade Brazil, are ousted in 1654

1640 — Portuguese recover their independence under John IV

1698 — Gold found in Minas Gerais

1725 — Gold found in Goiás

1729 — Diamonds discovered in Minas Gerais

1763 — Capital of Brazil moved to Rio de Janeiro

1777 — Treaty of San Ildefonso between Portugal and Spain roughly establishes boundaries of Brazil that hold until the present day

1789 — Unsuccessful revolt against the Portuguese

1808 — Portuguese royal court moves from Lisbon to Rio de Janeiro, which becomes capital of Portuguese empire

1815 — United Kingdom of Brazil and Portugal formed

1816 — Prince John becomes King John VI of Portugal, Brazil, and Algarves

1821 — João VI returns to Portugal, leaving his son, Dom Pedro, as regent in Brazil

1822 — Declaration of Brazil's independence; Dom Pedro becomes Emperor Pedro I

1824 — First Brazilian constitution

1825-1828 — War with Argentina; Uruguay becomes independent

1831—Abdication of the throne by Pedro I; his five-year-old son becomes monarch; regents govern from 1831-1840

1840—Dom Pedro II takes the throne at age fourteen

1851-1852—Brazil helps overthrow Argentine tyrant Manuel de Rosas

1865-1870—War of the Triple Alliance—Brazil, Argentina, and Uruguay fight against Paraguay; war ends with death of Paraguayan dictator Solano López

1888—Abolition of slavery

1889—Dom Pedro overthrown; republic proclaimed

1891—First constitution of the republic approved

1894—Brazil becomes stabilized; beginning of the First Republic

1917—Brazil enters World War I on the side of the Allies

1930—First Republic ends; government overthrown by Getúlio Vargas

1934—Second republican constitution adopted; Vargas elected president

1937—Revolt establishes the *Estado Novo* (New State); Vargas becomes dictator

1942—Brazil enters World War II on the side of the Allies

1945—Coup removes Vargas from power

1946—New constitution proclaimed

1950—Vargas again elected president

1954—Vargas forced to resign

1955—Juscelino Kubitschek elected president

1960—Brasília becomes new capital of Brazil

1964—Coup followed by military-backed government

1967—Fifth constitution of the republic adopted

1969—New constitution gives president broad powers; Lieutenant General Emílio Garrastazú Médici first president under this constitution

1974—General Ernesto Geisel takes office as president

1978—General João Baptista de Oliveira Figueiredo elected president; political reforms begin

1988—A new constitution is adopted restoring direct elections and changing the term of president from four years to five years; Brazil celebrates its 100th anniversary of abolition

1990—Fernando Collor de Mello is inaugurated as president; this is the first democratically elected regime in three decades

1991—Brazil's privatization program begins with the sale of a state steel company, Usiminas Siderugicas de Minas Gerais.

1992—Collor resigns from the presidency in December as he is indicted on charges of corruption and is impeached; Vice-President Itamar Augusto Cautiero Franco assumes the presidency; Brazil bids to host the year 2000 Summer Olympics.

1993—Congress passes legislation to pave the way for privatization of the nation's ports in efforts to expand exports through more modern and cost-efficient operations; dock workers launch a nation-wide strike to protest the expected reduced powers of the longshoremen's union.

1994—Congress endorses a $16 billion social emergency fund to be funded by taxes and other sources to curb inflation at 40 percent and balance the budget; the mayor of Rio de Janeiro bans the sale of guns in efforts to curb violence.

IMPORTANT PEOPLE

José de Alencar (1821-1877), novelist

Manuel Antônio de Almeida (1831?-1861), realist novelist

Castro Alves (1847?-1871), Brazilian poet, the "Poet of Slavery"

Jorge Amado (1912-   ), novelist who wrote about social problems

Pedro Àmérico (1843-1905), leading painter of the mid-nineteenth century

João Ataide, early mural painter

Aluísio de Azevedo, novelist who wrote about social change

Manuel Antônio Alvares de Azevedo (1831-1852), lyric poet

Pedro Álvares Cabral (1460?-1526), explorer who discovered Brazil for Portugal

Lúcio Costa (1902-   ), one of the chief architects of Brasília

Manuel da Cunha (?-1809), first known Brazilian portrait painter

Emanuel (1469-1521), king of Portugal at the time Brazil was discovered

João Baptista de Oliveira Figueiredo (1918-   ), general and president of Brazil from 1979 to 1985

Manuel Deodoro da Fonseca (1827-1892), first president of Brazil

Giberto Freyre (1900-1987), leading sociologist and anthropologist

Basílio da Gama (1740-1795), epic poet, best known for *O Uruguay*, a poem about the treatment of the Indians by the Spanish and Portuguese

Antônio Carlos Gomes (1839-1896), composer of operas in the Italian style

John VI (1769 or 1767-1826), king of Portugal, father of Dom Pedro I

Juscelino Kubitschek (1900-1976), president during the building of Brasília

Francisco de Lima e Silva (1785-1853), ruler of Brazil, 1831-1835

Jorge Mateus de Lima (1893-1953), mystic poet

Antônio Francisco Lisboa (1730-1814), artist of the colonial period

Francisco Solano López (1827-1870), Paraguayan dictator

Francisco Manuel, composer

Gregório de Matos Guerra (1623-1696), satirical poet

José Maurício (1767-1830), early composer

Victor Meireles (1832-1903), leading painter of the mid-nineteenth century

Oscar Niemeyer (1907-   ), one of the chief architects of Brasília

Francisco Orellano (1500?-1549), Spanish explorer who went up the Amazon in 1539

Pedro I (1798-1834), first monarch of independent Brazil

Pedro II (1825-1891), second monarch of independent Brazil

Philip II (1527-1598), ruler who united thrones of Spain and Portugal

Cândido Portinari (1903-1962), painter of War and Peace mural at the U.N.

Alberto Santos-Dumont (1873-1932), first man to construct and fly a gasoline-motored airship

Getúlio Vargas (1883-1954), dictator and president of Brazil

Heitor Villa-Lobos (1881-1959), famed composer

Presidents of Brazil

Marshal Manuel Deodoro da Fonseca, 1889-1891 (resigned)

Marshal Floriano Peixoto, 1891-1894 (acting president)

Dr. Prudente José de Moraes Barros, 1894-1898

Dr. Manuel Ferraz de Campos Salles, 1898-1902

Dr. Francisco da Paula Rodrigues Alves, 1902-1906

Dr. Affonso Augusto Moreira Penna, 1906-1909 (died in office)

Dr. Nilo Pecanha, 1909-1910 (acting president)

Marshal Hermes Rodrigues da Fonseca, 1910-1914

Dr. Wenceslau Braz Pereira Gomes, 1914-1918

Dr. Francisco da Paula Rodrigues Alves, 1918

Dr. Delphim Moreira da Costa Ribeiro, 1918-1919 (acting president)

Dr. Epitácio da Silva Pessoa, 1919-1922

Dr. Arthur Bernardes, 1922-1926

Dr. Washington Luiz Pereira de Souza, 1926-1930 (deposed)

Dr. Getúlio Dornelles Vargas, 1930-1945 (resigned)

Dr. José Linhares, 1945-1946 (provisional president)

General Eurico Gaspar Dutra, 1946-1951

Dr. Getúlio Dornelles Vargas, 1951-1954

Dr. João Café Filho, 1954-1955 (resigned)

Carlos Coimbra da Luz, 1955 (deposed)

Nereu de Oliveira Ramos, 1955-1956 (acting president)

Juscelino Kubitschek de Oliveira, 1956-1961

Jánio da Silva Quadros, 1961 (resigned)

João Belchior Marques Goulart, 1961-1964 (deposed)

Marshal Humberto de A. Castelo Branco, 1964-1967

Marshal Artur da Costa e Silva, 1967-1969

General Emílio Garrastazú Médici, 1969-1974

General Ernesto Geisel, 1974-1979

General João Baptista de Oliveira Figueiredo, 1979-1985

Tancredo Neves, 1985

José Sarney Costa 1985-1990

Fernando Collor de Mello 1990-1992

Itamar Augusto Cautiero Franco 1992-

INDEX

Page numbers that appear in boldface type indicate illustrations

About The Authors

Wilbur Cross, a professional writer and editor, is the author of some 25 non-fiction books and several hundred magazine articles. His subjects range widely from travel and foreign culture to history, sociology, medicine, business, adventure, biography, humor, education, and politics. He has touched on these and other subjects in the course of profiling the unique entity that is Brazil.

Mr. Cross worked for several years as a copywriter and was an associate editor at Life magazine. Married and the father of four daughters, he lives in Westchester County, New York.

A 1972 graduate of Bronxville Senior School, Bronxville, New York, Susanna Cross attended Ohio Wesleyan University and studied at the School of visual Arts in New York City.

Ms. Cross is president of FIRST FEATURES, Inc., a marketing and communications company she recently founded in Nashville, Tennessee. She is also an independent songwriter, and the co-author of NASHVILLE FEVER, a romance novel that was serialized in more than 100 newspapers through Universal Press Syndicate.

J
981   Cross, Wilbur.
C   Brazil.